LAW SCHOOL AND BEYOND:

THE IHS GUIDE TO CAREERS IN LEGAL ACADEMIA

—— 2ND EDITION ——

CONTRIBUTORS:
Tom Bell
David Bernstein
Scott Bullock
Paul Edwards
Richard Epstein
Claire Hill
Andrew Morriss
John Moser
Erin O'Hara
David Price
Brett Scharffs
Eugene Volokh
Stephen J. Ware
Ashlie Warnick
Todd Zywicki

Law School and Beyond: The IHS Guide to Careers in Legal Academia - 2nd Edition
Copyright © 2008 by the Institute for Humane Studies
All rights reserved.

TABLE OF CONTENTS

Foreword by Richard A. Epstein 1

PART 1 – BEFORE LAW SCHOOL
Choosing a Law School – David Price 7
Preparing for Law School – Paul Edwards 9

PART 2 – IN LAW SCHOOL
Succeeding: Grades, Networking, and Law Review – John Moser 15
Making Law Review and Making it Work for You – Ashlie Warnick .. 19
Writing a Student Article – Eugene Volokh 25
Making the Most of Your Summers – Todd Zywicki 33
Choosing a Specialization – Tom Bell 35
Should I Consider a Joint JD/PhD? – Paul Edwards 37

PART 3 – AFTER LAW SCHOOL
Clerkships – Stephen Ware and Todd Zywicki 41
Publishing – Andrew Morriss 46
Publicizing Your Work – Eugene Volokh 49
Legal Practice – John Moser 51
Fellowships – Erin O'Hara 52
Advanced Law Degrees – Claire Hill 54

PART 4 – THE JOB MARKET
Some Observations and Predictions – Brett Scharffs 55
Approaching the Job Market – Stephen J. Ware 58
The AALS Process – Andrew Morriss 59
The AALS Faculty Recruitment Conference – Andrew Morriss 65
Common Meat Market Questions – David Bernstein 72
The Campus Visit – Brett Scharffs 73
Public Interest Law as a Career – Scott Bullock 78

Appendix I: Legal Academic Career Bibliography
and Useful Web sites 86
Appendix II: Success Factors in Legal Academic Careers:
Some Survey Data 90

Acknowledgments 95

FOREWORD

Entering, and Excelling in, Law School Teaching[1]
Richard A. Epstein, *University of Chicago Law School*

I have just had the privilege of reviewing the materials that the Institute for Humane Studies has assembled to help students, especially (but not exclusively) those of a classical liberal orientation, make their way into legal education. I am glad that I do not have to run the gauntlet today. When I entered into legal education over thirty years ago as a young legal cub of twenty-five, the process was more informal and less exhausting than it is today.

I took my initial teaching position at the University of Southern California right after graduating from Yale in 1968. My initial contact with USC was an interview at Yale with George Lefcoe, followed by an on-the-spot invitation to visit the school, which I did a couple of weeks later. No job talk, only an exhausting round of non-stop interviews, ending late at night in a singles bar. An offer followed the next week, which was promptly accepted. The deal was wrapped up before December 1st of my senior year.

One interview, one school, one offer, one month.

Today, matters are obviously different. To begin with, law schools have rightly abandoned the practice of hiring students right out of law school. Now, a clerkship (which I did not have) seems to offer a big edge, especially when followed by a snazzy job in the Solicitor General's office, a Washington agency, or with a fancy law firm. Multiple degrees are often required and publications beyond a law review comment are close to a must. The job search involves multiple visits to multiple schools, as candidates and schools search for just the right match.

---

[1] Foreword taken from *Law School and Beyond: The IHS Guide to Careers in Legal Academia* (1st ed. 1999).

This pronounced shift stems from a mixture of happy and sad reasons. On the positive side, the standards within the profession have surely risen. Law schools demand more from their young faculty, and therefore have to spend more time in vetting candidates. On the negative side of the ledger, more process is an attempt to overcome fundamental disagreements as to what constitutes a strong job candidate. My own libertarian instincts were pretty apparent even in 1968, and they raised more than one eyebrow at USC, which, like most law schools, was dominated by centrist Democrats steeped in the legal process tradition. The span of intellectual orientation and political belief was much narrower than today—the centrist democrats of an earlier age have dwindled in numbers.

Today, law schools are the home to faculty with strong worldviews and political ideologies. Classical liberals and law and economics scholars are included in the mix, but it is not news to report that law schools are also home to feminists, critical race studies specialists, and communitarians of all stripes and sizes. This wide divergence in sentiments about sound legal scholarship makes it necessary to take refuge in an ever-longer hiring process in order to broker the differences between worldviews that all too easily coalesce into factions. It is not uncommon to watch faculty struggle with appointments by following an updated version of the Missouri compromise: take one from your group, and one from ours. But these compromises often prove unstable. You can make two offers and gain but one acceptance. What then?

In an atmosphere of distrust, it is no easy matter to extend deals over multiple periods when changes in external conditions, university finances, and faculty composition all conspire against it. All in all, the political landscape is far more complex than the one I encountered in 1968. Yet, my advice to any applicant, including any classical liberal, is exactly what the IHS guide recommends: ignore the political undercurrents, and explain your position candidly to those who disagree with you—no evasions, no resentments, no fulminations. You are going to have to learn to work with people with whom you have fundamental disagreements. Start early.

How, then, to negotiate the process? One key is to understand the odds that you face. Candidates for teaching positions have gone through many job interviews with firms, where the best strategy is to sit tight and wait for the offers to roll in on the strength of a sterling résumé. It does not work that way in academia. No longer is the presumption that every job interview will result in a job offer. Now the number of applicants exceeds the number of positions by a factor of five or ten. Law firms may hire sixty students per class; large law schools are not likely to hire more than three or four entry-level people in one year. So you have to distinguish yourself from the pack.

That means taking prudent risks in interviews. It means going the extra mile to prepare yourself. It is not good enough to express an interest in teaching intellectual property. You should read the leading casebooks on the subject and explain why you incline to choose one over the other; you should know the recent major decisions in the area, and review them before the interview; you should keep up with legislative activities and leading articles. You should read the newspaper on recent developments. You should be prepared to talk on matters pertaining to your specialty and matters of general interest. You should consciously plan an agenda of matters to talk about in the interview so as to avoid those awkward silences between a pointed question and a brief answer.

You have to be the focal point of conversation; you have to keep the flow of the conversation moving so that your interviewers stop thinking in the role of interviewer and get engaged in the conversation for its intrinsic intellectual merits. You have to make them feel as though their cherished opinions are at risk. The passive strategy may land you in the middle of the pack; but the middle of the pack does not get offers in today's market. You have to work to rise to the top, and take the risk that you may fail miserably at your first choice because of an unhappy luck of the interview draw.

But should you try to run this gauntlet at all? Teaching is not for everyone. Reading this IHS guide will give you the best collection of advice on how to move from start to finish in the job search. It rightly emphasizes that the process begins with the first day of law school, and that the coveted positions go to people who consistently pursue their goal with single-minded determination. But it does not, and perhaps cannot, tell you whether you will thrive in the pathless forests of academe. This business is not for every law school graduate with an IQ of 150 and an impeccable set of credentials. Those qualifications might get you in the door, but standing alone, they will not make for a great scholar.

That requires a peculiar set of personal temperaments, skills, knacks, and intuitions, which are harder to coach, but which in the long run will determine your academic success. It is hard to describe exactly what these are, but it is possible to give some hints as to the things that you should look for in yourself when deciding whether or not to embark on a legal academic career.

The first point is cautionary: success is not tied to any one personality type. Flashy and mercurial types may do quite well; but so do solemn, cautious types, and everything in between. Law is big enough and varied enough to offer a home to just about everyone. What really matters is the level of passion and commitment that you bring to the job. The young professors who succeed in teaching are those for whom learning counts both as consumption and investment. They love their work. They are curious about everything. They do not have any narrow or mechanical definition of relevant knowledge. They build quite consciously on their undergraduate education, and store away nice points that have the habit of becoming relevant as they focus in on particular problems. They care about both doctrine (yes, doctrine) and practice. They think that legal rules and social institutions matter. They worry about outcomes, and they worry equally about the rigor of the argument that leads to said outcomes. They care about how everything connects, about how commitments made in one area impinge in unsuspected ways on another. They have strong intuitions about right and wrong, but are willing to modify or abandon those intuitions in the face of strong arguments to the contrary. They are willing to face down a crowd to defend their beliefs, but to yield to a single pointed objection that they cannot answer. They don't worry too much about being popular or being liked. They like being respected for their integrity and honesty. And in the midst of all the world's pressures, they develop a consistent intellectual agenda that governs their research over the long run.

The ablest professors that I know always have more topics on which to write than they have time. Each article segues neatly into the next. I give this brief portrait, for I think that it covers most of the great scholars whom I have been privileged to know in more than thirty years of teaching. I also mention it because it is critical that you know in advance that many excellent students only become excellent professors if they have passion, drive, focus, curiosity, independence, fortitude, and ambition to work on a continuous basis after they land their first teaching position. Teaching and researching in law has been for me the dream of a lifetime come true. Legal academia is a lifetime occupation that gives its greatest rewards and satisfactions to those who sustain their intellectual vitality over the long haul. You have to decide whether you fit this profile. And if you do, then the IHS guide is the place to turn to help you obtain your initial faculty position, which is the sine qua non for all the good things that can follow from a successful academic career.

PART 1: BEFORE LAW SCHOOL

Choosing a Law School
David Price, *Institute for Humane Studies*

You might have found that picking an undergraduate school was hard. You, like many of your peers, went on road trips with your parents to visit campuses. There, you were led by personable tour guides from the admissions office who walked backwards as they pointed out campus landmarks. Then you went back home and pondered whether you wanted a big research university or a small liberal arts school, a college town setting or an urban one, a warm climate or a snowy one, and many other factors.

Your choice of law schools should be much simpler. If you are serious about a career in legal academia, you should be concerned with the prestige of the school and little else. In the larger scheme of things, three years is a short time to put up with bad weather, a less-than-idyllic setting, or whatever other issues might deter you from going to the highest-ranked school that accepts you.

IHS survey research supports the intuition that legal academia, like much of the legal profession, is a land of labels; the status of a candidate's law school plays a very large role in faculty hiring—both directly (as a major factor in faculty interview invitations) and indirectly (as a major factor in clerkship hiring).

General rankings of law schools by popular outlets such as *U.S. News and World Report* are suggestive, but imperfect, measures of a school's status. Brian Leiter, a professor at the University of Texas School of Law, has developed a number of analytically more sound law school rankings centered on issues including faculty quality, student quality, and job placement, which are available at his Web site, *www.leiterrankings.com.*

Of particular relevance to the prospective law teacher is Prof. Leiter's ranking of law schools as feeders into legal academia. This ranking is based on his analysis of the educational background of tenure-track—but untenured—faculty at 63 well-regarded law schools, including the top 50 law schools as determined by *U.S. News and World Report*. By focusing on not-yet-tenured faculty, Prof. Leiter was able to derive information on which schools have been contributing the most new law professors in recent years (not just ten or twenty years ago).

In addition to looking at the overall number of a school's alumni who landed teaching positions, he also considered the size of the school's entering classes (to avoid giving advantage to large schools); the quality of the appointments obtained; and the frequency with which a school's graduates had the benefit of an additional degree, such as an LL.M. or a graduate degree in another field, before obtaining their appointment.

Because the differences in the schools' outcomes were sometimes too small to be truly meaningful, given the other factors at work, Prof. Leiter eschewed the straight numerical rankings beloved by editors of news magazines. Instead, he took the seventeen schools showing the most success in producing law teachers and he divided them into five groups. Schools in group 1 enjoyed the most success in producing law teachers, schools in group 2 were the next most successful, and so on.

The results of Prof. Leiter's study are set out below with his kind permission.[2] Schools are listed alphabetically within each group.

GROUP 1
Yale Law School

GROUP 2
Harvard Law School
Stanford Law School
University of Chicago Law School

---

[2] Source: Brian Leiter's *Law School Rankings*, available at www.leiterrankings.com

GROUP 3
Columbia Law School
New York University School of Law
University of California, Berkeley Boalt Hall School of Law
University of Michigan Law School

GROUP 4
University of Virginia Law School

GROUP 5
Cornell Law School
Duke University School of Law
Georgetown University Law Center
Northwestern University School of Law
University of California, Los Angeles School of Law
University of Minnesota Law School
University of Pennsylvania Law School
University of Texas School of Law

Preparing for Law School
Paul S. Edwards, *Mercatus Center at George Mason University*

University students who want to go to law school inevitably ask, "What is the best undergraduate curriculum to prepare for law school?" They are usually frustrated to learn that there is no one best program of study. The simple fact is that law schools admit students from a variety of academic disciplines. What may be true, however, is that in addition to demonstrating mastery of your undergraduate academic discipline, you will be best served in law school by putting together a broad and challenging undergraduate curriculum that emphasizes research, writing, and analysis.

For example, if you study English literature, a strong undergraduate preparation for law school would include some rigorous courses in philosophy, economics, and political science. Furthermore, depending on when you read this advice, you might think strategically about what kind of undergraduate training will best help you in the future. So, for example, if you want to do serious academic work in commercial law, corporate law, or bankruptcy, you should understand microeconomic theory, organizational behavior, and financial and cost accounting. Similarly, if you are interested in constitutional law, you should become conversant in both positive political theory and normative political philosophy, and so forth. In real life, it happens that students who are well-versed in discrete subjects are usually drawn to a substantive legal specialization that makes good use of their well-developed skills and interests. At the same time, keep in mind that grades are important; don't sacrifice your GPA for an "interesting" class.

THE LSAT EXAM

Whatever substantive curriculum you choose, you will need to take the Law School Admissions Test (LSAT), and have strong letters of recommendation. Plan to take care of both in good order early in your college career.

The LSAT is offered four times each year—June, September, December, and February. Deadlines for registering are generally one month in advance of the testing date. The LSAT Web site (www.lsat.org) offers a great deal of information about the process, and allows users to register online, review sample questions, and receive test scores. Strategically, it is best to take the LSAT in the summer between your junior and senior year rather than try to fit it into the fall term of your senior year. Not only does this give you some time to prepare for the test, but should something go wrong during the examination, you can cancel your score and retake it in the fall. Commercial preparation courses (such as Stanley Kaplan) are well worth their price, if only because they familiarize you with the demands of the test and provide an incentive to prepare.

The LSAT Web site is also the best place to register with the Law Schools Data Assembly Service (LSDAS). Nearly all law schools require that you use this service, which collects your application materials (scores, transcripts, letters of recommendation, etc.) and sends them to the law schools to which you apply.

Early in your college career, you should target professors who can provide you with good letters of recommendation. These should be respected scholars who have shown some interest in your own work and ideas. Cultivate a relationship with these professors by taking advantage of (but not abusing) office hours and look for opportunities to work for them as research assistants. The ideal letter of recommendation comes from someone who can write that you did well in his or her class, and can write knowingly and specifically about your character. When it comes time to solicit letters, ask your professors explicitly what kind of letter they could write for you and whether they are able to give you a top-notch recommendation. It may be an awkward thing to ask, but it is much better than trying to get into law school with letters from reluctant professors. Once they have agreed, give them plenty of advance warning and information. Generally, you should give your letter writers a copy of your résumé, your transcript, a writing sample, and a copy of your personal statement. You should always waive your right to see the contents of your letter of recommendation! Candid letters are taken far more seriously than ones that the subject has read.

The conundrum of how best to prepare for law school is a uniquely American problem. In most countries, legal education is an undergraduate curriculum. One of the peculiar features of modern American legal education is that law is, chronologically speaking, a graduate program—admittance requires an undergraduate degree. But functionally, law is more like an undergraduate curriculum inasmuch as it is an introductory course. In theory, no one in the large introductory first-year law school courses of contracts, torts, civil procedure, property, criminal law, or constitutional law has an advantage over anyone else because of prior academic training. Therefore, it is probably best to avoid undergraduate "legal studies" courses and concentrate on getting a solid grounding in the social sciences and humanities. Law professors like to reserve to themselves the initiatory rites of passage into the study of law.

Your first day of law school begins with the assumption that the room is filled with smart individuals from a variety of backgrounds with a legal tabula rasa. Don't believe it. Many first-year law students arrive with a fairly good outline of the substantive areas that they will be studying that year. Even more arrive with very clear goals about what they want to accomplish while at law school (Order of the Coif, law review, judicial clerkship) and how best to achieve those goals. So without prejudicing the unique approaches that your law professors will bring to the subject matter, allow us to suggest a handful of pre-law school strategies that will give you the upper hand in your important first year of law school.

No year of law school is as important as your first year. Decisions about membership on the school's law review, decisions about your second-summer law firm clerkship, and decisions about judicial clerkships are all based largely on the academic record made during your first year. So, even if you "catch on" later in the game, and accumulate a strong academic record in your second and third year, not as many important gatekeepers will have an opportunity to recognize your talent. Moreover, your first year establishes a substantive foundation for all other classes that follow at law school. The specialized commercial law courses of your second and third year assume that you understand contracts; the specialized regulatory classes assume that you understand torts, criminal law, and constitutional law; and any moot courts or clinical courses assume that you understand basic procedural law. You need to know the importance of the first year going into law school so that you can pace yourself accordingly. The first year of law school is a sprint with big prizes for the winner. If you want the acclaim of law review and prestigious clerkships, then first year is not a time to pace yourself. Go for broke, recognizing that there are ways to rest and breathe later.

First, get a good overview of the terrain prior to running the race. You would not want to run a year-long sprint without first stretching and jogging the course. Thankfully, there are a number of ways to warm up. Although you will absolutely need to learn the skill of reading cases and placing them into a doctrinal framework, there is no problem with getting an overview of the doctrinal framework first. All law school bookstores are filled with commercial outlines of the law. The naïve law student will turn to these resources in the weeks prior to exams as a way to cram. You should turn to these resources during the summer prior to law school, not as a replacement for the tough and necessary work of grappling with each of the cases as they come up during the school year, but as a way of anticipating and framing that exercise.

Second, learn early on about your professors, particularly their scholarly and pedagogical styles. As soon as you know who your professors will be (by calling the law school during the summer), run a simple bibliographic search on Legal Trac and then look up their major articles. This will give you a strong sense of what your professors value.

Third, learn some basic legal research prior to taking your law school legal research and writing course. Although you may not have access to the increasingly important electronic legal databases (Lexis and Westlaw), understanding the format of the standard bound references in legal bibliography and their relationship to one another will give you an upper hand in knowing how best to access cases and statutes.

Finally, an important note for your first week at law school: Many law school libraries keep previous law school exams on file. Look up previous exams during the first week of school—not the week before the exam. As you go through your courses, keep the questions from your professors' prior exams at the front of your mind, constantly asking yourself how today's cases and analysis would apply to those previous exams.

SUMMER PRIOR TO LAW SCHOOL BIBLIOGRAPHY

- Jacques Barzun, *Simple and Direct*. Chicago: University of Chicago Press, 1994
- Stephen Elias and Susan Levinkind, *Legal Research: How to Find and Understand the Law* (5th ed.). Berkeley, CA: Nolo Press, 1997.
- Robert Ellickson, Order *Without Law: How Neighbors Settle Disputes*. Cambridge, MA: Harvard University Press, 1991.
- Richard Epstein, *Simple Rules for a Complex World*. Cambridge, MA: Harvard University Press, 1995.
- Lawrence M. Friedman, *A History of American Law*. New York: Simon & Schuster, 1973.
- Henry M. Hart, Jr., and Albert M. Sacks, *The Legal Process: Basic Problems in the Making and Application of Law*. Westbury, NY: Foundation Press, 1999.

- Herbert Jacob, *Law and Politics in the United States*. Boston: Little, Brown, 1986.
- Karl Llewellyn, *The Bramble Bush: On Our Law and Its Study* (8th ed.). New York: Oceana Publications, 1985.
- Richard K. Neumann, *Legal Reasoning and Legal Writing: Structure, Strategy, and Style* (2nd ed.). Boston: Little, Brown, 1994.
- Richard Posner, *Economic Analysis of Law* (4th ed.). Boston: Little, Brown, 1992.
- William Strunk and E.B. White, *The Elements of Style* (3rd ed.). New York: Macmillan, 1979.

PART 2: IN LAW SCHOOL

Succeeding: Grades, Networking, and Law Review
John Moser, *Ashland University*

GRADES

There are three keys to making the most of your years in law school. First, and most important, is high grades, which are important for a number of reasons. Your first-year grades will, in large part, determine whether you will make law review and get a good clerkship. High grades will also affect your ability to network successfully with your professors—there will be more on this later. But there is another reason why high first-year grades are vitally important, though it is more subtle and psychological. Professors and students alike have reported that in the first year, often by the end of the first semester, something of a caste system begins to emerge in law classes. The top students—the ones who will go on to do really big things—will begin to recognize one another and choose to spend time together. You will want to be a part of this group, and not just because it's nice to fit in with a good crowd. These are the people who, most likely, will be running the law review, and this can help you to win an editorship. But even beyond that, they will also serve as your network after you leave law school. Knowing the right people is of tremendous benefit in any line of work, and legal academia is no different.

So, how does one go about getting good grades? Much will depend on your own basic intelligence, your talent for taking tests (not always the same thing as intelligence), your capacity for hard work, and your ability to manage your time. This guide will not help you with any of these, but there are a few strategies that may help improve your grades. Taking old exams (your law school, most likely, will keep these on file) is one method of preparing; nothing prepares for an exam like a dry run or two, or three. Study groups are another common tactic, and are also helpful in developing networking relationships with your fellow students. Another useful strategy is simply to get to know your professors.

This sort of information-gathering pays many dividends. It will certainly give you a head start in the crucial networking process, but more immediately it will suggest how to conduct yourself in class. Does Professor Smith have a reputation for holding a particular point of view? If so, is she fair—or known to dismiss opposing viewpoints as naive or dangerous? If you make classical liberal arguments in her class, how is it likely to go over?

Moreover, to the extent that it is possible for you to choose your classes, you might want to avoid courses taught by those known to be tough graders—or at least push such courses off until the third year, when grades are less crucial. This may seem like a cheap way of getting your grades up, but when the time comes for people to make decisions about you (law review editorships, clerkships, jobs), high grades are what they'll be looking for. Another piece of advice for the first-year law student is to not take on any new responsibilities that might distract you from your work. If you can possibly avoid it, don't work—even part-time—except perhaps as a research assistant. Moreover, you are well-advised to postpone getting married, having a child, or doing anything else that is potentially disruptive.

NETWORKING

The second key to maximizing the value of your law school years is networking. Part of this, as I mentioned above, involves associating yourself with other talented peers. It is not a good idea to wall yourself off from peers who do not share your philosophical orientation. Throughout your life, you will have to work with people who do not agree with you, and as a law professor, this will certainly be the case. Make a reputation for yourself as a thoughtful person who engages others' views constructively, not an ideologue who thinks he has all the answers. Your ability to command the respect of your peers, even those who disagree with you on practically everything, can make all the difference between success and failure in an intellectual career.

Although networking with your peers is important, your primary goal ultimately should be to develop relationships with your professors. In addition to learning about their work and their classroom demeanor, find out early which ones have a reputation for supporting students.

Ideally, you will want to develop a mentoring relationship with one or more faculty members (the more distinguished the better) who are willing and able to promote young scholars. In traditional academic programs, a graduate student chooses a dissertation advisor with whom he or she will work closely over the next several years; there is then the presumption that the advisor will assist the student in getting an academic job. Of course, there is nothing like this in a typical JD program. Therefore, it is up to you to make connections and try to establish relationships.

It is not a good idea to let networking wait until your second year. At the very least, you should be making sure that the professors who teach your classes know who you are right now. Approach them at the podium after class (with moderation—you don't want to gain a reputation for being a pest), visit them during their office hours (again, within moderation), invite them to lunch, or find other opportunities to speak with them. Students often feel as though such approaches are an imposition, but law professors (like most people) love to talk about themselves and their work. Once you've read Professor Smith's most recent article on torts, go find Professor Smith and ask her some questions about it. She'll not only be flattered, but will remember you as a person who is interested in ideas in general, and her ideas in particular. Of course, you must make sure you have something intelligent to say!

Once you've made the initial connections, strengthen those relationships as your law school career continues. After your first-semester grades come out, make a special approach to the professors who awarded you the highest grades. In the middle of your second year, you'll be applying for clerkships, and for that, you'll need solid letters of recommendation. A professor who knows you only from your performance in one of his classes might be willing to write a letter on your behalf, but that letter won't be nearly as good as one written by a professor with whom you've spoken on numerous occasions.

As your relationships with faculty members develop, find other opportunities for closer interaction. Explore the possibility of working as a research assistant for your mentor. Also, in your second and third years, you may register for independent study courses, allowing you to work one-on-one with a professor (this is a good way to write something for law review as well). And by all means, maintain your connections with the faculty after you graduate; they will be some of your most important allies when you go on the job market.

However, don't limit yourself to making contacts within your law school. Consider the wider world of legal academia. Pay attention to what is being written in the best law journals. If you read an article that you find particularly interesting, challenging, or important, take a moment to send the author a thoughtful letter or an e-mail. Even if you don't receive a response, there's one more person who might recognize your name (and associate it with something good) at some point in the future.

You should also take the opportunity to develop relationships with law professors with a classical liberal bent and similar scholarly interests. This is another area where organizations such as IHS and the Federalist Society can be of tremendous assistance. Tell them what you're interested in, and these groups can let you know about legal scholars working in the same areas. Such faculty members are often looking to make connections with like-minded law students, particularly students who are on law review. These contacts can be rewarding, not only professionally, but personally as well. After all, it's always nice to communicate with those in your field who share your philosophical outlook.

At the same time, it's very important to have relationships with professors who are not classical liberals and who will write letters on your behalf. A job candidate who comes recommended by more than classical liberals or conservatives will stand out as a scholar rather than as an ideologue.

LAW REVIEW

The final element in making the most of law school is participation in your school's law review, which is precisely what Ashlie Warnick addresses in the next section.

Making Law Review and Making it Work for You
Ashlie Warnick, *Yale Law School*

WHY LAW REVIEW?
Being a member of your school's law review sends a powerful signal to the academic world.

First, it shows that you work hard, are a superior writer, and had excellent grades in your first (and toughest) year of law school.

Second, it suggests that you know what good legal scholarship looks like. While many authors submit their pieces to the highest-ranked journals, only a few are selected. By learning to recognize the difference between mediocre articles and top-notch ones, your own academic writing will benefit, and hiring committees will be more likely to think that you can publish in the top journals.

Third, it demonstrates that you can play well with others. Being a faculty member is more than publishing a paper or teaching a course. You will also mentor students, serve on committees, and attend and contribute to faculty meetings, all of which require social skills and collegiality. Furthermore, your fellow faculty members will look to you to help improve their scholarly works (as you should look to them). A successful stint on law review shows that you can interact with others in a positive way.

HOW TO GET ON LAW REVIEW
So, with all the benefits that law review provides, how do you become a member? Because each school is different, you should find out about your particular school's selection process as soon as possible during your first year. That said, there are some trends: While a few schools base membership solely on students' first-year grades, most require all applicants to participate in a "write-on" competition.

In this competition, which usually begins in late spring following the semester's exams, all applicants will be assigned a particular legal topic where all source materials are provided to you and outside research is not permitted. You will then be asked to research and write either a case comment or a student note (a shorter and more narrowly-defined student-written article) on the chosen topic. In most cases, you will have three to four weeks to submit your work, at which time it will be blind-graded by the incoming editorial board.

The key to success in this competition is to prepare and start early. In the spring semester, before the competition even begins, read student notes or case comments published in the law review. These will give you an idea of the format and style that the editors want to see in your work. Once the competition begins and you pick up the assigned research materials, read them over and budget plenty of time to familiarize yourself with the topic area. The better your understanding of the law, the more well-reasoned and persuasive your submission will be.

No matter how persuasive your first draft might be, it is not done yet. Even though writing your 25-35 page submission can eat up large amounts of time, make sure to leave time to go back and edit it. Polish the language and correct any niggling errors that might have crept into the document. It seems unthinkable, but each year, a handful of students submit their write-ons with incomplete sentences, unmatched verb tense, spelling mistakes, etc. Needless to say, such mistakes will not improve your chances of success. When grading, board members will look not only at the content of your submission (i.e., its persuasiveness and how it deals with counterarguments) but also at whether the sources it references are properly cited and whether it reads like a law review piece.

Lastly, make sure to carefully read and follow the instructions for the competition. Many competitions have strict instructions about submission length, page numbering, margin size, and citation format. While these requirements may seem like tedious details, failing to meet them could result in the board giving your submission a lower score or rejecting it outright. Better to take the time to turn in a conforming submission than rue it later.

HURRAY, I WAS ACCEPTED. NOW WHAT?

It's been several weeks since you turned in your submission, but you heard back and found out you made it. Congratulations! Now that you are a junior or associate member of your school's law review, you will most likely be tasked with a lot of cite-checking. When cite-checking an article, associate members make sure that its footnotes are formatted correctly and that they accurately reflect the source material. Although not particularly exciting work, it is necessary.

However, being an associate member is not all drudgery. During this time, you will also begin working on your own scholarly project, such as a Student Note or a Case Comment (hereinafter, simply "Note"). Some law reviews do not require their associate members to write a Note and, as a result, very few students do. This means that if you do finish your Note, you are virtually assured that it will be published. This is a great opportunity to get your first publication on your CV.

At other schools, the Note process is not quite as optional. There, all junior members must complete their Note before they may become full members of the law review during their third year. This means that the law review will simply not have sufficient space to publish each and every finished Note. If your law review is like this, selecting the right Note topic becomes extremely important. You must pick something that is timely, but not in danger of being pre-empted; something that is interesting, but not so interesting that it has already been done; something important enough to warrant scarce journal space but not so large and complex that you cannot complete it in the required time frame. To successfully navigate this maze, you should talk to your favorite professors (both past and present), ask your 1L summer employer, and read through new legal publications. If you spend the summer finding, perfecting, and narrowing down your topic, you will be well ahead of your compatriots come the fall.

Writing a Note can be a large undertaking, so break it down into manageable bites. Set aside time each week to work on your Note and meet regularly with your assigned Note Editor to get his or her feedback. This is critical for multiple reasons. First, your Note Editor can often provide you with valuable guidance. Second, when the Notes Editors meet to discuss your work, your Note Editor's opinion will carry considerable sway in how others regard the piece. And third, your Note Editor is a member of the Editorial Board who will vote in the upcoming Editorial Board elections. So play nice, take criticism graciously, and incorporate his or her comments as much as you can without losing your own voice. Your piece will be stronger for it and you will get credit as someone who can work well with others.

I GOT A TASTE OF LAW REVIEW LIFE AND WANT MORE. HOW DO I RUN FOR EDITORIAL BOARD?

As you may have guessed, academic employers see serving on the Editorial Board as an even stronger signal of quality. It not only demonstrates that you care about legal scholarship as a consumer, but that you are willing to be an active part of the production process. While Editorial Board elections are generally competitive in that there are more applicants than available positions, being selected is possible with planning and effort.

In the late winter/early spring of your second year in law school, the outgoing Editorial Board will meet to select the following year's Board. But just as with your write-on submission and your Note, preparation is key. There are several ways to improve the odds.

The Editorial Board selection meeting can be, to some extent, a popularity contest, so make sure that the current Editorial Board thinks of you as personable and pleasant. Producing a quality journal is a group effort, after all. Throughout your first year on Law Review, get to know the current Editorial Board members. Ask them about their own personal views, what their Editorial Board positions are like, and how they think the journal could potentially be improved. In this same vein, be polite to your fellow students (whether on the review or not). Rude or obnoxious behavior—even off campus—will not be forgotten.

Second, be mature and professional in your law-review tasks. Did you complete your cite-checking assignments on time? Did you do a good job on them? Did you work diligently to solve an Article's problems on your own before leaving it to the Article Editor to fix? Did you volunteer to help the Symposium Editor with the logistics of the review's symposium? Were you polite and did you interact with professors at the symposium? The more you can truthfully answer "yes" to these questions, the more you will persuade the Editorial Board that you can be trusted with one-on-one, ongoing contact with authors.

Finally, forge a good working relationship with your Note Editor and make steady, solid progress on your Note. Respond positively to your Note Editor's criticisms and suggestions and, just as with your cite-checking assignments, be sure to meet your Note Editor's deadlines. Your Note Editor will most likely be the person in the selection meeting who has had the most face-to-face time with you, so his or her opinion can make or break your candidacy.

OK, I'VE PREPARED. WHICH POSITION SHOULD I RUN FOR?

So by this point, all members of the Editorial Board should think of you warmly as a charming, diligent member of the team. Now that the selection meeting is nigh, you will be asked to tell the Editorial Board what positions you are interested in. Above all else, choose positions in which you have a genuine interest. That said, some positions are more valuable than others for those pursuing an academic career:

The Editor-in-Chief (EIC) is obviously the most valuable position for those planning academic careers. The EIC oversees the entire law review, including article selection. He or she routinely interacts with authors and serves as the face of the law review with the faculty. But there can be only one EIC and competition for the position is often fierce.

Among the remaining positions on the Editorial Board, those with some responsibility for the journal's contents, such as Article Editor or Book Review Editor, are generally more valuable for those interested in academia. These positions also let you work closely with authors, making suggestions about how the piece can be improved. The relationships you form with scholars through these positions can also be useful to your own writing.

Another valuable Editorial Board position is Symposium Editor. This person, sometimes with the assistance of the EIC, the Articles Editors, and a committee, puts together a group of scholars to visit your campus and present articles on a single legal topic, which are subsequently published as a single issue of your journal. Although this position involves a great deal of autonomy and exposure because the Symposium Editor plans and coordinates both the symposium and its resulting issue of the journal, you should be aware that some reviews only conduct symposia every other year. This position is less rewarding if you hold it in the "off-year."

A less valuable, though still valuable position, would be Note Editors who assist fellow students in completing their Notes. Note Editors do not have an opportunity to interact with outside scholars, but do play a significant role in shaping the student-written work that is published in the journal.

Lastly, a few words about the remaining Editorial Board positions—Managing Editor, Executive Editors, etc. These positions involve the actual production process of the Law Review. The Managing Editor, although usually the second name on the Law Review masthead, is not really an editorial position. Instead, the Managing Editor oversees the business end of production. Executive Editors are generally in charge of proofreading the final versions of an issue before it goes to press and assigning and monitoring the cite-checking assignments given to associate editors. Even though any Editorial Board position is better than none for CV building, you may be better off if you spend the time you would have devoted to these positions to writing your own scholarly work. Publications, after all, are likely more impressive to hiring committees than holding an administrative position on your law review's Editorial Board.

Writing a Student Article[3]
Eugene Volokh, *UCLA Law School*

A well-written student article can get you a high grade, a good editorial board position, and a publication credit. These credentials can, in turn, help get you jobs, clerkships, and—if you're so inclined—teaching posts. The experience will hone your writing, quite likely a lawyer's most important skill. And some student articles actually influence judges, lawyers, and legislators; even the U.S. Supreme Court cites student works several times each year.

Writing a student article, whether as a law review note or as an independent study project, is also one of the hardest things you'll do in law school. Your non-law writing experience and your first-year writing class will help prepare you for it, but only partly. Creating an original scholarly work that makes a contribution to our understanding of the law is not easy.

In this section I try to give some advice, based on my own writing experience, for you to mix and match with whatever other advice you get. These ideas have worked for me, and I hope they work for you. If you find this article useful, I suggest you reread it at various stages of your project; as you get further into your piece, you might find yourself profiting from some tip that you missed when you first read it.

Good legal scholarship should meet the requirements of patentability: It should (1) make a claim that is (2) novel, (3) nonobvious, and (4) useful. It should also (5) be seen by the reader to be novel, nonobvious, and useful.

---

[3]The following is extracted from a longer article of the same name and is used here with the author's permission. This excerpt deals specifically with the importance of publishing, as well as some tips on selecting a suitable topic. The complete article is available at http://www.law.ucla.edu/faculty/volokh/writing.htm. Mr. Volokh is also the author of *Academic Legal Writing: Law Review Articles, Student Notes, and Seminar Papers* (Foundation Press, 2007).

A. THE CLAIM

Most good works of original scholarship have a basic thesis: a claim that they are making about the world. You should be able to condense that claim into one sentence, for instance:
- "This-and-such a law is unconstitutional."
- "The legislature ought to enact the following statute."
- "Properly interpreted, this statute means this-and-such."
- "My empirical research shows that this law has unexpectedly led to...."
- "Viewing this law from a [feminist / Asian studies / Catholic / economic] perspective leads us to conclude that the law is flawed and should be changed in such-and-such way."

Some articles, for instance some historical pieces, quite properly fall outside this mold, but they are the exception rather than the rule.

How do you find a worthy claim? First, find a problem that interests you. Think back on cases you've read for class; did any of them make you think "This leaves an important question unresolved" or "The reasoning here is really unpersuasive"? Read recent Supreme Court cases and see whether they leave major issues open, or perhaps create new ambiguities or uncertainties. Try to recall class discussions that intrigued you but didn't yield any well-settled answer. Most casebooks include questions after each case—many of these flag interesting and unsolved problems.

Ask practicing lawyers which important unsettled questions they find themselves facing. Ask faculty members which areas of the law they think are fertile sources for ideas; some professors (though not all) may even suggest specific problems. If you want some tips, check out Heather Meeker's thorough and useful "Stalking the Golden Topic: A Guide to Locating and Selecting Topics for Legal Research Papers," 1996 *Utah Law Review* 917.

Choose a problem that's big enough to be important and interesting, but small enough to be manageable. Turn the problem into a five-word title; if you can imagine a book with that title (e.g., "Bankruptcy: A Sociological Perspective"), the problem is too big.

Second, run your chosen problem by your faculty advisor. The advisor will probably know better than you whether the problem has been definitively resolved, or whether there's already been too much written on it, or whether there's less there than meets the eye.

Third, do your research with an open mind; be willing to make whatever claims your research and your thinking lead you to, and even be willing to change or refine the problem itself. You might, for instance, initially decide to write about restrictions on speech by sitting judges, but as you do your research decide that it's more interesting to write about restrictions on speech by candidates for judicial office.

Fourth, decide what seems to be the best solution to the problem. Depending on the problem, it could be a new piece of legislation, or a new constitutional or common-law principle, or a specific application of a general principle to a certain kind of case, or an explanation of why judges behave as they do. This will be your claim: "The solution to the problem is ____"; "the law should be [this-and-such]"; "this law is unconstitutional in these cases, but constitutional in those."

Test your solution against several factual scenarios you've found in the cases, and against several other hypos you can come up with. Does the solution yield the results that you think are right? Does it seem determinate enough to be consistently applied by judges and juries? If the answer to either question is "no," try to refine your claim to make the answer "yes."

The solution doesn't have to be perfect; it's fine to propose a solution even when you have misgivings about the results it will produce in certain cases. But candidly testing your solution against the factual scenarios will give you an idea whether even you find the solution plausible. If you don't, chances are your readers won't, either.

Your claim—your proposed solution—will probably change as you think still more about the subject, as you do more research, and as you write. That's good; always be open to making your claim more correct or more nuanced or more defensible.

B. NOVELTY

To be valuable, your article must be novel: It must say something that hasn't been said before. It helps if your claim itself is novel, but at the very least your claim coupled with your basic rationale must be novel.

For instance, say you want to argue that obscenity law is a bad idea. Believe me, it's been done to death; no novelty in the claim. You might want to find something less overwritten.

Still, you're OK if you can come up with a novel justification for your claim. For instance, the claim that "obscenity law is a bad idea because recent empirical studies show that it's usually enforced primarily against political or ethnic minorities" may well be novel.

What if you've chosen your topic and your basic rationale, and four weeks into your research have found that someone else has said something that's basically the same? No need to abandon ship just yet.

Often you can make your claim novel by making it more nuanced: For instance, don't just say "obscenity law is a bad idea," but say (perhaps) "laws banning distribution of obscenity are a bad idea unless the obscenity describes acts that are themselves unconsented and criminal, such as child molestation or rape." The more complex your claim, the more likely it is that no one has said it before. Of course, you should make sure that the claim is still (a) useful and (b) correct.

Some tips for making your claim more nuanced:
1. Think about what special factors—for instance, government interests or individual rights—are present in some situations covered by your claim but not in others. Could your claim be modified to take these factors into account?
2. Think about your arguments in support of your claim; do they work well in some cases but badly in others? Perhaps your claim should be limited or softened accordingly.
3. For most legal questions, there's an intuitive "yes" answer and "no" answer; both tend to attract a lot of writing. See if you can come up

with a plausible answer that's somewhere in between— "yes" in some cases, "no" in others.

C. NONOBVIOUSNESS

Say Congress passes a law creating a federal cause of action for libel on the Internet. You decide to write about how such a law doesn't violate the First Amendment.

Your thesis would be novel, but pretty obvious. If you discuss it with most people, they'll say, "Yeah, you're right, but I could have told you that myself." Libel law, if properly limited, has repeatedly been held not to violate the First Amendment, and many people have already argued that libel law should be the same in cyberspace as outside it. Unless you can explain how federal cyber-libel law is relevantly different from state libel law applied to cyberspace, your point will seem banal. Articles that just apply settled law—or familiar arguments—to slightly new fact patterns usually look obvious.

You can avoid obviousness by adding some twist that most observers would not have thought of. For example, might federal cyber-libel law be not just constitutional, but also more efficient, because it sets a uniform nationwide standard? Could it be more efficient in some situations but not in others? Could there be some unexpected interaction with some other federal laws? Making your claim more nuanced can make it less obvious as well as more novel.

A good way of checking for obviousness: Run your thesis past a faculty member (besides your advisor) who works in the field, past an honest classmate, past a lawyer who works in the field—if you don't know one, ask your advisor to refer you to one—and past a smart layperson.

D. UTILITY

You'll be investing a lot of time in your article. You'll also want readers to invest a bit of time in reading it. It helps if the article is useful—if at least some readers can come away from it with something that will be professionally valuable.

Focus on Issues Left Open: Say you think the U.S. Supreme Court's Doe v. Roe decision is flat wrong. You can write a brilliant piece about how the Court erred, and it might be useful to some academics. But Doe is the law of the land, and unless the Court revisits the issue, few lawyers will practically benefit from your insight. You should ask yourself: How can I make my article more useful, perhaps useful to lawyers and judges as well as scholars?

One possibility is to identify a point that Doe left unresolved, and explain how it should be resolved in light of Doe's reasoning, along with the reasoning of several other Supreme Court cases in the field. Now that would be useful to anyone who's litigating a question that involves the unresolved issue.

Apply Your Argument to Other Jurisdictions: Say that Doe holds that a certain kind of police conduct doesn't violate the Fourth Amendment. This makes Doe binding precedent with regard to the Fourth Amendment, but only persuasive authority as to state constitutions—state constitutions need not be interpreted the same way as the federal one. The thesis "State courts interpreting their own state constitutional protections should reach a different result" is thus much more useful than just "the Court got it wrong." Judges are more likely to accept the revised thesis, and lawyers are more likely to argue it. Your article will still be valuable to scholars who evaluate the Court's case law, but it'll also be valuable to many others.

Consider Making a More Politically Feasible Proposal: Say your claim is quite radical, and you're pretty sure that few people will buy it, no matter how effectively you argue it. Say, for instance, that you want to urge courts to apply strict scrutiny to restrictions on economic liberty—a step beyond even Lochner v. New York. Even if you have a great argument for that, you should understand that few courts will be willing to adopt your theory.

Think about switching to a more modest claim. You might, for instance, argue that courts should apply strict scrutiny to restrictions on entry into certain professions or businesses. This would be a less radical change, and you can also support it by using particular arguments that wouldn't work as well for the broader claim.

Maybe courts will still be unlikely to go that far. Can you argue for a lower (but still significant) level of scrutiny? Can you find precedents, perhaps under state constitutions, that support your theory, thus showing your critics that your theory is more palatable to courts than one might at first think?

Or perhaps you could limit your proposals to strict scrutiny for laws that interfere with the obligation of contracts, rather than for all economic restrictions. Here you have a stronger textual argument, a narrower (and thus less radical-seeming) claim, and perhaps even some more support from state cases—it turns out that the Contracts Clauses of state constitutions are often interpreted much more toothily than the federal one.

If you really want to make the radical claim, go ahead; you might start a valuable academic debate, and sometimes radical claims carry the day. On the other hand, especially for student articles, practicality is quite important. By making a more modest claim, you can remain true to your basic moral intuition while producing something that's much more likely to influence people. Many a campaign—and especially many a legal campaign—is most effectively fought through small, incremental steps.

E. THINGS TO AVOID

1. *Articles that show there's a problem, but don't give a solution.* Giving a solution makes your article more novel, nonobvious, and useful, and generally turns it into a better professional calling card. You want to show people that you have a fine, creative legal mind that can solve problems as well as discover them.

2. *Case notes.* An article that describes a single case and then critiques it is likely to be fairly obvious, even if it's novel and useful; and it doesn't show off your skills at research and at tying together threads from different contexts. If you got your topic from a particular case, keep it; but don't focus on the case, focus on the problem, and bring to bear all the cases that deal with the problem.

3. *Articles that just explain what the law is.* These can be useful, and sometimes even novel, but they tend to be obvious—the reader is

likely to say "True, I didn't know this, but I could have figured it out if I just sat down and did a bit of research." Just fine if your reader is a busy lawyer looking for a good summary of the law; not so good if your audience is a professor, a law review editor, or a judge looking for a law clerk.

4. *Responses to other people's works.* Framing your article as a response to Professor Smith's article will limit your readership to people who've already read Smith's article and will tend to pigeonhole you (fairly or not) as a reactive thinker rather than a creative one. If your piece was stimulated by your disagreement with Smith, no problem—just come up with your own claim and prove it, while demolishing Smith's arguments in the process. By all means cite Smith in the footnotes; Smith's opposition will help show that your claim is important and nonobvious. But don't let Smith be the main figure in your story.

5. *Excessive mushiness.* Be willing to take a middle path, but beware of proposals that are so middle-of-the-road that they are indeterminate. For instance, if you're arguing that single-sex educational programs should neither be categorically legal nor categorically illegal, it might be a mistake to claim that such programs should therefore be legal if they're "reasonable, fair, and promote the cause of justice." Such a test means only what a judge wants it to mean.

Few legal tests can produce mathematical certainty, but a test should be rigorous enough to give at least some guidance to decision-makers. Three tips for making tests clearer:

a) If possible, tie your test to an existing body of doctrine by using terms of art that have already been elaborated by prior cases.

b Whenever you use terms such as "reasonable" or "fair," ask yourself what you think defines "reasonableness" or "fairness" in this particular context.

c) When you want to counsel "balancing," or urge courts to consider the "totality of the circumstances," ask yourself exactly what you mean. What should people look for when they're considering all the circumstances? How should they balance the various factors you identify? Making your recommendation more specific will probably also make it more credible.

Thus, "single-sex educational programs should be legal if they're narrowly tailored to an educational approach that's been shown effective in controlled studies" is probably a more defensible claim than "single-sex educational programs should be legal if they're reasonable."

CONCLUSION

Getting published can help you become a better writer, and thus a better lawyer. It can help you become a more successful lawyer, by getting you a good grade, a good board position, a publication credit, and the clerkships, lawyer jobs, or teaching jobs that can flow from this. And it can, even if only slightly, influence the law for the good.

Making the Most of Your Summers
Todd J. Zywicki, *George Mason University School of Law*

So you've made it through your first year of law school. Congratulations! Now you can kick back, relax, and enjoy the summer, right? Not so fast. True, during your first summer, you have a degree of flexibility that you probably will never have again. During the summer after your second year, you'll be working at a law firm, and the summer after that will be spent preparing for the bar exam. But that only makes it all the more important that you spend that first summer as productively as possible. And there are much better things you could be doing than waiting tables.

One very good option for this summer is to try to arrange a judicial internship. Many federal judges (though certainly not all of them) bring one or more law students on board for a summer to serve as research assistants for their clerks. If you can manage this, it will pay off in numerous ways. First of all, it will give you a connection to a federal judge that can repeatedly help you in your career. It will undoubtedly help you land a good post-law school clerkship; while many judges hold to a policy of not hiring their own former interns as clerks, they will certainly give you recommendations (assuming you did a good job!). The experience will also give you needed practice in legal research and writing, and may give you ideas for law review notes or articles.

There usually isn't a standard procedure for applying for a judicial internship. The best way to approach this is to write a letter to a judge for whom you'd like to intern. And if you know someone who is clerking for a judge, you can try to set something up through him or her.

The big problem, however, is that such internships are almost never paid positions, so even if you do manage to set up an internship, you'll have to find outside funding in order to support yourself for the summer. There are fellowships available for this purpose, so check with your placement office, or search the internet for possibilities.

There are a number of other productive ways in which you might spend your first "free" summer. Working as a research assistant for one of your professors is a worthwhile option, although faculty often spend large parts of the summer away from the office. Working for a law firm or a government agency such as the U.S. Attorney's Office can also give you valuable experience. If possible, try to write a student note for law review—this will pay lasting benefits throughout your career.

As I mentioned previously, you'll be expected to spend the summer between your second and third years of law school working at a firm. The goal here is to show that, all academic knowledge aside, you have what it takes to be a lawyer. Unlike clerkships, which require a certain amount of initiative on your part to set up (see the section on "Clerkships" below), getting a summer job at a law firm is a fairly simple proposition. Early in the fall of your second year, the placement office at your law school will collect students' résumés and periodically post lists of firms that are recruiting from that school. You will then be able to choose the firms with which you'd like to interview. The key here is to choose "blue chip" firms, preferably in Washington, D.C., or a major commercial center such as New York City. These are the sorts of firms that potential academic employers will regard favorably.

If you've followed the basic advice offered here so far—been accepted into a top law school, earned high first-year grades, and joined the staff of the law review—you should have no problem getting a job at a prestigious firm. Once you're there, expect to work very hard, and very long hours. You want to impress your bosses enough that they will give you an offer to work there after you have completed law school and your clerkship(s). Nevertheless, if you can, try to take at least a couple of weeks off during the summer (before your job begins, or after it's over) to work on some academic writing.

Choosing a Specialization
Tom W. Bell, *Chapman University School of Law*

Because law schools often hire to fill particular curricular needs, specialization can give you an edge on the job market. Even during your first year of law school, when required courses monopolize your schedule, you should start thinking about future areas of concentration. In your second and third years, when you have more freedom to choose your classes, learn all that you can about a few particular topics. Keep your specialization strategy in mind when you pick the professors with whom you network, the sort of law you practice, and the topics on which you will write before going on the academic job market. In all these ways you can bolster your claim to valuable, specialized knowledge.

How do you choose a specialty? Begin by surveying your interests and aptitudes. Choosing an area of specialization that bores you would invite a fairly miserable (and probably unsuccessful) academic career. What legal topics most excite your attention? The ones that most aggravate you may inspire a zeal to reform. Others may attract you with coolly logical puzzles.

In what scholarly pursuits do you excel outside of law school? Perhaps you enjoy the natural sciences; if so, consider focusing on environmental law. If you enjoy financial studies, corporate or tax law might suit you well. Happily, you can aim at combining work with pleasure.

However, you should look beyond the intrinsic appeal of specialty if you want to pursue a teaching career. Choosing the right specialty at the right time can dramatically increase your chances of finding academic employment. Think like an entrepreneur, looking for important areas of law in which relatively few academics work.

Opportunities for academic arbitrage often appear in expanding areas of law, in the train of technological or political innovation. Gaps for new academic entrants can also open up in areas of practice that pay a great deal more than academia can offer, or simply in areas that scholars have thus far overlooked. By way of example, law schools have in recent years sought candidates who can teach intellectual property, international trade, corporate, or tax law. Pick a winning specialization, and you increase your odds of landing an academic job.

It may pay to develop a specialty even if you plan to research and write in other fields. Practicing intellectual property licensing may, for instance, qualify you to teach contract law. Hiring you might then appeal to a law school on the market to replace a retiring teacher, even as you plan to publish works on copyright law.

On the other hand, some specializations may hurt your chances for academic employment. So many would-be academics want to specialize in constitutional law, for example, that only a very few of the very best actually get a chance to do so. Classical liberals, in particular, should think twice before trying to squeeze into those fields, because their ideas will quite likely displease the current majority of law professors. Nor does it pay to rely solely on arcane specialties, such as legal history or law and literature, which will support no more than a seminar every couple of years. Better you should focus on specialties that will sell on the job market—the specialties that schools can use.

Such practical advice may have you crying, "But I live for admiralty law!" However, you need to get hired before you can indulge your obscure scholarly cravings. In the meantime, while on the job market, you should try separating your research interests from your teaching interests. All but a few top law schools require new faculty to help teach the most popular classes. Most schools really do not care what you write about, though, so long as you publish in quality and quantity. By saying, "I'm qualified to teach contracts and business organizations, but I plan to research and write on Internet law," you show yourself both useful to your colleagues and appropriately interested in legal arcana.

In addition to choosing an area of specialization, you might also consider associating yourself with a particular school of thought or methodology. A school may be hiring for a "law and economics person," after all, or for some other type of scholar. You need not ally yourself with any movement, however; a promising professor can stand on her own two feet. Associating with the wrong crowd might even set you back. But you might very well choose wisely in affiliating yourself with a well-respected and lively group of academics.

In that event, learn the literature of the movement and make contacts with its most important adherents. Think about how you might contribute to their ongoing discussion. Can you resolve apparent conflicts, summarize extant scholarship, or answer old questions? Take care to fit your scholarly contributions into contexts, and frame them with respect. Your well-crafted efforts may make you friends, make your name, and make you successful in landing an academic job.

Should I Consider a Joint JD/PhD?
Paul S. Edwards, *Mercatus Center at George Mason University*

The best law schools in the country attract students who have strong undergraduate records and therefore have many options. Inevitably, one of those options is specialized graduate study in the same (or closely related) field as their undergraduate major. Students with a strong academic orientation and interests in law often wonder what, if any, is the value of combining a JD with a PhD as a way of maximizing their academic credentials.

Although professors with both a JD and a PhD are an increasingly common presence on law school faculties, the opportunity costs associated with adding a PhD are so high, and the benefits are still so unclear, that it is best to exercise extreme caution in deciding on this route. What follows is a frank discussion of the advantages and disadvantages of pursuing a PhD with a JD. The following discussion assumes that the PhD under consideration is in the social sciences or humanities, not the natural sciences.

The advantages to earning a PhD along with a law degree are that you gain strong research and writing skills and unique substantive expertise that can lead to a fertile research agenda. Also, if you ever wish to work within a university faculty other than a law school, you must have a PhD. On the other hand, the time you spend working toward that degree may well keep you from other legal experiences, and you run the risk that your substantive overspecialization may actually make you less desirable for law faculty purposes.

Before discussing the pros and cons of pursuing a JD/PhD, it is important to understand a few things about law school and university faculty hiring. Law schools typically screen candidates through the Association of American Law Schools (see Section 4.3). The prototypical law faculty candidate finished at the top of her class at a top law school, served on the law review editorial board, published a student note, clerked for a prestigious court, and while practicing law at a top law firm, published a substantive law review piece. Granted, there are many variations to this track, but this is roughly the prototype.

University faculty hiring is fairly routinized through the major professional associations of the disciplines. Announcements for openings are made through the profession's newsletters. The candidate is in the difficult and solitary process of completing a highly specialized dissertation that is being supervised and endorsed by a committee of scholar-specialists as making an original contribution to scholarship in that discipline. The best candidates have already published a peer-reviewed article or two in their discipline and have an established record as a research assistant and teaching assistant. Again, there are many variations to this prototype.

This rough outline should help you see that even the simple logistics of law school and graduate school are not entirely consistent. In other words, only the exceedingly rare individual can fare well in both settings. If you turn from a completed JD to the arduous work of completing a dissertation, you will likely forgo the clerkship and law firm associate experience that are highly valued at law schools.

Nevertheless, if done well, a PhD will give you unsurpassed training in how to conduct original research in the social sciences or humanities. Law school will provide you with some good research skills, but they are mostly internal to the law (*i.e.*, they rely on standard legal sources and bibliography). A social scientist who understands how to frame and test hypotheses with sound empirical methods, and who further understands how to fit those methods to the substantive concerns, can make enormous contributions to our understanding of the law. Someone grounded in the literature and reasoning of moral philosophy, who also understands the law, can contribute significantly to normative legal philosophy. And in the field of law and economics a background in statistics and economic theory can be a tremendous asset. A PhD, then, if done well, can give you better methodological training that will allow you to analyze legal problems from important external perspectives.

Nevertheless, for the young legal scholar, a PhD is neither necessary nor sufficient for getting a law faculty position. While it may enhance your substantive qualifications, it is not a substitute for doing very well at law school and gaining some important legal experience. Moreover, some senior law faculty remain suspicious of what your hyperspecialization in an outside field can contribute to law, other than to criticize and obfuscate. Consequently, if law school teaching is your aim and you are considering a PhD, you must assure yourself that the time and effort involved in getting a PhD (which is significant) do not detract from good law school grades and garnering substantive legal experience.

For those still not dissuaded from pursuing both degrees, there are some strategic considerations for how best to proceed. If law school teaching is your aim, it may be to your advantage to complete most of the requirements for the PhD (including the dissertation) prior to starting law school. This gives you the added credential, but puts the required law school experiences at the top of your CV. If the PhD follows the JD, then you should try to garner some strong practical legal experience (*i.e.,* take a year off for a judicial clerkship), and make your dissertation highly relevant to the law. Also, be certain that you have chosen a graduate program with faculty who understand and support your desire to go into law teaching. Never forget that academic politics is rife with explosive issues of status, prestige, and professional jealousy, and not all university faculties will support your decision to teach in a law school.

For all the generic advice offered, you must ultimately rely on what you understand to be your unique comparative advantage. If you feel that your comparative advantage can be honed through joint study, and you have the time and resources to do it well, investigate that option thoroughly and deliberately. It is a high risk/high reward strategy, and it is obviously not for everyone.[4]

---

[4] Editor's note: This issue is also addressed in Appendix II, p. 92.

PART 3: AFTER LAW SCHOOL

Clerkships
Stephen J. Ware, *University of Kansas School of Law*
Todd J. Zywicki, *George Mason University School of Law*

A judicial clerkship is one of the most important credentials for an aspiring legal academic. Many law professors served as clerks after law school and the experience of clerking is probably more similar to being a professor than almost any other practice experience. A connection with a federal judge, and the experience of writing legal opinions, are both assets that will serve you well in your job search. And as with choosing a law school or a firm, you'll generally want to get the best clerkship that you can.

At the top of the clerkship hierarchy, of course, is the U.S. Supreme Court. Given that there are only nine Supreme Court justices, however, there are not many clerkships at this level to go around, and are thus extremely competitive. It is certainly possible to get an academic job without having served as a clerk on the Supreme Court, so don't panic if you aren't selected for one, but if you can manage it, you'll have a credential that will open doors for you at some of the nation's best law schools.

In any case, it is quite rare for anyone to get a Supreme Court clerkship straight out of law school. Typically, students arrange during the fall of their third year to clerk for a federal judge upon graduation, then (assuming they're successful) apply for a Supreme Court clerkship during the spring of their third year of law school. Frequently, people apply during the year of their first clerkship, or even during their first year or two of legal practice. Most likely, then, you'll be applying for your first clerkship early in the fall semester of your third year of law school. During your second year of law school, you should familiarize yourself with the following Web sites: http://www.cadc.uscourts.gov/internet/lawclerk.nsf and https://lawclerks.ao.uscourts.gov/.

The first Web site is an overview of the Federal Judges Law Clerk Hiring

Plan and the second is a list of job openings and an indication about which judges—now, the vast majority—are participating in the Hiring Plan. The main purpose of the Hiring Plan is to defer clerkship decisions until the third year of law school. (When the authors were law students, clerkship applications, job offers, and acceptances all occurred during the second year of law school. Most everybody thought that was too early.)

At the time of this writing, the Hiring Plan states, "Law clerk applications from third year students, and letters of reference on their behalf, may not be sent before the day after Labor Day." It also claims that, "Judges may not conduct interviews or extend offers before the third Thursday after Labor Day."

Those considering an academic career should aim for a federal circuit court clerkship. There are also clerkships available with federal district courts and state courts, but these are less likely to be valuable credentials and experience for a later teaching position. Many law professors were federal circuit court clerks at some time, and they often look for similar credentials in making hiring decisions.

There are roughly 180 Federal Circuit Court judges scattered through thirteen circuit courts around the country, and unlike the search for summer jobs with law firms, you must apply individually to each judge with whom you'd like to clerk. Which ones should you choose? The most important consideration should be reputation among law professors. First of all, some circuits are more prestigious than others; the D.C. Circuit is at the top of the list. Talk to your professors for guidance here. Find out where other students at your school have managed to clerk in the past, and then take into consideration your own standing among your classmates.

Beyond that, do some research on individual judges. Are they widely cited as legal scholars? Certain judges are respected so highly that clerkships with them are as highly regarded as D.C. Circuit clerkships. Moreover, clerkships outside the Northeastern corridor and large cities around the country are often less competitive than those concentrated in legal centers with many law schools. Thus, you should apply broadly and be flexible as to where you are willing to live for the one or two-year period of your clerkship. Indeed, even those reluctant to move to less popular locations often find that they enjoy the opportunity to live in an unexpected location for a year.

Equally important is the question of which judges have a history of helping their clerks move on to bigger and better things. Some actually have reputations as feeder judges, meaning that their clerks tend to go on to Supreme Court clerkships. Some of the same judges have many professors among their former clerks. Two former clerks of the same judge share a bond, even if they are a generation apart.

You might also want to pay some attention to the issue of philosophical compatibility. Both the Federalist Society and IHS can offer names of prestigious judges who are openminded or even sympathetic to classical liberal ideas.

For how many clerkships should you apply? There is no upper limit here, but realize that there is only a limited amount of time available (usually only the second half of September, although some judges go later) in which to schedule interviews. And then, of course, there's the financial constraint—if a judge chooses to bring you in for an interview, you will be expected to bear the costs of travel and lodging during your visit.

By the end of the spring semester of your second year, you should know to which judges you'll be applying for clerkships and should have at least a couple of professors lined up to write your letters of recommendation. Over the summer, you should spend some time putting together your applications. Each judge may have his or her own requirements, but for the most part, the application will consist of a cover letter, résumé, transcript, writing sample, and recommendations.

Generally, judges conduct interviews during the second half of September and often start making offers immediately. Most judges use four main criteria when deciding which candidate to hire:

1. Academic record (law school, grades, participation on law review)
2. Personality (that is, basic compatibility with the judge)

3. Recommendations
4. Philosophical outlook.

Don't limit your campaign to your application alone. If you have contacts who are clerking during the year you are applying, or even know someone who has a friend who is clerking, you should do your best to exploit that connection and get the clerk to put in a good word. A call to IHS or the Federalist Society may get you names of current clerks who might be in a position to help you out. Also, note that some professors limit the number of students that they will recommend in any year, so it is important to get to know your professors well and to contact them early in the process about your interest in having them serve as a recommender.

In addition, you can increase the possibility of securing a clerkship through other credentials that may make your application stand out. For instance, some judges have internship programs for students while in law school or during summers in law school. Working as an intern for a judge, especially as a full-time summer intern, may help your application stand out and may also help you navigate the application and interview process more knowledgeably. Working for a professor or interning in the federal government may also be credentials that distinguish you from the crowd.

When scheduling interviews, it is important to remember that offers are generally made within a day or two of the interview and sometimes even at the end of the interview itself. Moreover, judges will want an answer as soon as possible. They may not even give you a day or two to accept. Therefore, it is wise to formulate a ranking of preferences for clerkships, and plan your interview schedule accordingly. If you get a call from the secretary of a judge who is relatively low on your list, try to schedule the interview as far in the future as you can. By contrast, if your top choice calls, get there as soon as you can. Ideally, you'll want to get an offer from your first choice before interviewing elsewhere, thus saving on travel expenses.

When interviewing with a judge, keep several things in mind. First, the judge will only be choosing three or four clerks, so he or she can afford to be picky. Your job is to distinguish yourself from the pack and sell yourself as the perfect clerk for that judge. Do some research—read a few of his or her opinions on topics that interest you. When you are able to discuss these in your interview, this will demonstrate your enthusiasm as well as your respect for the judge's jurisprudence.

Second, the relationship between judges and clerks is an intimate one, so the judge will place a premium on personal compatibility. Therefore, it is imperative that you be polite and friendly toward everyone you meet—and this means not only the judge, but his staff as well. If the secretary remarks to the judge about you, "What a nice young person," your chances will go up. You will most likely interview with the judge's current clerks as well and they often provide substantial input into the judge's decision. Third, clerkship interviews are often quite substantive, rigorous, and intellectually intense. In many instances, the interviews with the judge's current clerks may be more intellectually intense than the interview with the judge.

You may hear at your school that protocol demands that you do not turn down an offer of a clerkship. This is not necessarily true; the expectation varies, so talk to your professors about the judges with whom you'll be interviewing. That way, if a judge calls shortly after the interview to make an offer, you will know whether he or she expects immediate acceptance during that phone call. Usually, you will be expected to respond fairly quickly (within 48 hours). This means that there will not be time to do more interviewing before you make your decision (although you can and should use the time to make calls to other judges with whom you've already interviewed, but heard nothing), so strategic scheduling of your interviews is of the utmost importance. Turning down a clerkship offer might not always be a breach of etiquette, but if you do so in the absence of an offer from somewhere else you could be taking a serious risk.

Once you've begun your clerkship, there are a few things to keep in mind. Obviously, you'll want to do your best to impress the judge—this is a contact that will help you throughout your career. Do all you can to learn about the judge before the clerkship begins; certainly, you should read all of his or her opinions that you can get your hands on. This will help you, when writing legal opinions, to write in the judge's voice. It will also help you avoid writing an opinion that may contradict one of his or her earlier opinions.

Also, remember that you work not only for the judge but also for his or her permanent staff, including the secretary. Because such staff members generally control access to the judge, the clerk who fails to pay them sufficient respect will often suffer for it. Finally, you should make sure to enjoy the experience—maximize your opportunities to attend oral arguments and to meet the clerks in other chambers, many of whom will become friends and even future academics as well.

One other bit of advice: between the time you leave law school and the time you start teaching, the clerkship will be the closest thing you will have to a nine-to-five job. Use your free time to your advantage, working on a paper for publication in a law review. The rich variety of cases that come across your desk will often provide fodder for future law review articles and will raise many interesting legal issues, and typically questions that are more interesting than you are likely to encounter once you are in practice.

Publishing
Andrew P. Morriss, *University of Illinois College of Law*

If you plan to become a law professor, you must begin to publish like one long before you actually enter the job market. Hiring committees at the majority of law schools care a lot about your potential as a scholar, and the best predictor of future production of scholarship is a solid track record of publishing. Successful faculty candidates tend to have more pre-job market publications than unsuccessful ones, so this is an important step.

Publishing before you become a member of a law faculty has its own unique challenges. First, your employer may have an opinion about whether or not you should be writing academic pieces; this time-consuming activity may be interpreted as a lack of commitment to your current professional duties. Judges and law firms, in particular, often have rules about the topics on which you can publish while employed. Find out what those rules are before you start writing. Second, without faculty colleagues, you won't have ready sources of advice about the submission process or for critiques of your work. The advice in this guide can help with the former; but for the latter, you need to build a network to assist you. Ask your friends to read drafts, contact faculty from your law school for advice, and ask IHS for assistance in finding reviewers to offer comments. If you or a friend regularly blog on legal topics, get a mention of the paper into the blog. Most importantly, arrange to post a working paper version of your article on the Social Science Research Network (www.ssrn.com), where it will reach an academic audience.

There are literally hundreds of law reviews—almost 500 of varying types at the time this was written. With that many journals, you are likely to be able to publish your article somewhere. Of course, publishing in a prestigious journal is preferable, although very difficult. One top 20 law review's faculty adviser recently told me that his journal gets 3,000 submissions a year and seriously considers fewer than 100, which means that journals will make very quick decisions about most of the submissions, often relying on rules of thumb about the status of the author. As a non-faculty author, you will be at a disadvantage because of your status.

There are three types of scholarly legal journals: (1) general interest, student-edited law reviews; (2) special interest, student-edited law reviews (e.g. *Environmental Law, Texas Journal of International Law*); and (3) faculty-edited, peer-reviewed journals. Unless you have an advanced degree in a social science, it will generally not be worth submitting to the peer-reviewed journals, as they require that you submit to only one journal at a time, tend to use non-*Bluebook* citation formats, and have longer review processes. Nonetheless, if you believe your piece might fit one of those journals, you should talk to faculty friends to determine if submission to one is appropriate.

Among the student-edited journals, the best placement is a top general interest law review. Placing a piece in one of these journals, however, is very difficult; therefore, you should consider the specialty journals as well, particularly those affiliated with elite law schools or specialized practitioner's bar (e.g., the *Administrative Law Review*, the *Energy Law Journal*).

Publication in a top specialty journal is more impressive than in a mediocre general-interest law review.

For student-edited journals, submissions tend to be clustered around the time the editorial boards change (between late February and early May, depending on the school) and late July/early August, when articles editors return from their summer clerkships. Pieces submitted outside these windows can get successful placements, of course, but the vast majority of articles are sent during these times.

Consider using an electronic delivery service to make your submission. ExpressO (http://law.bepress.com/expresso/), for example, will submit your cover letter, resume, and manuscript to those journals you select for a modest fee. Several journal editors have told me that they prefer such submissions, because it makes distributing the materials to the law review staff simple. Some journals, however, do not accept electronic submissions at all.

Regardless of how you deliver your manuscript, the package should include a professional-looking version of your article, complete with running headers in a law review style and *Blue Book* citations, your resume, and a cover letter summarizing your qualifications and explaining the article concisely—*i.e., less than one page*! Make a list of the law reviews to which you've submitted your article, along with contact information for the review.

Opinions vary greatly among faculty about the optimal submission strategy. Some prefer to send their articles in waves, starting with a top group and then gradually adding additional schools. Others submit to their entire list at once. Some submit to elite journals only, others submit to a larger pool. My advice to a non-faculty author is to submit to the top 100 (ranked by the most recent *U.S. News & World Report* rankings) plus the relevant specialty journals in a single wave. Doing this maximizes your chances of a quick offer to get the process started. However, you should discuss strategies with your faculty mentors to get additional opinions.

Whichever strategy you prefer, your goal is to generate an offer and then "trade up" to a better placement. Typically, you will be contacted by a law review interested in publishing your piece and given a short period to respond (one to two weeks is the norm; be sure to negotiate for as large a window as possible). Thereafter, immediately begin calling more highly ranked law reviews to inform them that you have an offer and therefore need an expedited review before your deadline. (If you used ExpressO for submission, the service allows you to handle this electronically for some law reviews, although you should follow up with a phone call as well.) Don't immediately call the *Harvard Law Review* when the number 75 school's journal makes an offer—work your way up through the ranks in stages. The *HLR* will be more impressed by an offer from *Texas* or *Northwestern* than by one from *Oregon*. When you get another offer, repeat the expedite process with the next group of higher ranked journals, once again negotiating as large a decision period as possible.

Publishing is important. But the key element to establishing your career is to publish good work. Make sure that the research and analysis in your pre-tenure track articles reflects your best possible efforts. Law professors excel at picking holes in things, and your work is likely to be read carefully by both members of appointments committees, and their colleagues if you get to the call-back interview stage. Moreover, your publications may signal your politics and so harm your candidacy. Think carefully about the topics of your pre-market publications. If you plan a piece on *The Virtues of Clarence Thomas's Originalism,* you should probably wait until later to publish it. Articles that make creative use of empirical evidence or historical materials tend to be less ideologically charged and therefore effective pre-market scholarship for aspiring law professors.

Publicizing Your Work
Eugene Volokh, *UCLA Law School*

[The following is an excerpt from Eugene Volokh's article, *Writing a Student Article,* used here with the author's permission. The complete article is available at http://www.law.ucla.edu/faculty/volokh/writing.htm.]

Once your piece is published, you want people to read it or at least to know that it exists. Even people who don't read your article might think more highly of you if they know you've published something.

Order at least 100 reprints, though more is better. Reprints tend to run from thirty to seventy cents for each extra copy beyond a minimum number, so splurge.

Then, distribute copies, with a descriptive cover letter, to:

1. All law professors at your school whose work is remotely connected to your area.

2. All legal professionals who have helped you (did you thank them in your author's note?)

3. All legal professionals whom you cite in your footnotes. Mention in your cover letters where you cite them. Everyone likes to see their names in print.

4. All lawyers you know who work in the field, even those you only met in passing while working as a summer associate.

5. All law professors who write treatises and casebooks in the field. Their addresses are in the Association of American Law Schools (AALS) Directory of Law Teachers, found in the library.

6. Any judges who are deciding cases to which your article is relevant, and lawyers who are litigating such cases, and any law firms or other organizations that might litigate such cases in the future.

7. The offices of any legislators, lobbyists, or political groups that are interested in any legislation to which your article is relevant.

8. Anyone else whom you might want to impress.

9. Anyone else who might be in a position to help you spread your ideas. (Editor's Note: IHS falls under this category!)

Ideas that get actively promoted are more likely to get adopted. People who actively (but tastefully) promote themselves are more likely to get jobs, either immediately or down the road.

Legal Practice
John Moser, *Ashland University*

After your clerkship, but before you go on the academic job market, you will most likely spend several years working for a law firm or a government agency. Although the actual amount of time spent in this way will vary from person to person, the average will be between two and five years. Working less than two years will create the impression that perhaps you don't have what it takes to be a lawyer. On the other hand, spending more than five years outside of an academic setting may lead potential employers to question how serious you are about scholarship.

In most cases, you will take a job at the same firm where you worked during the summer between your second and third year of law school. This will save you the trouble of having to look for a job during your third year or your clerkship. However, if an opportunity beckons at a more prestigious firm or government agency, you may want to trade up.

As for choosing a job, the same guidelines apply as for the summer job. You'll want to pick a high-prestige firm, preferably one located in a major city, such as New York, Washington, D.C., or Los Angeles. All things being equal, you'll probably want to go with a firm that works in your specialized area of law. Talk to your professors or your placement office for advice in this regard.

Another possibility is to work for the government, but you need to exercise quite a bit of caution here. The government employs thousands of lawyers, but most of them occupy positions that have virtually no chance of leading to an academic career. Becoming a prosecutor or a bureaucrat in some federal agency, for instance, is probably a dead-end academically speaking, as are most positions in state or local government. However, there are some federal offices that are highly regarded by law schools. The U.S. Attorney's Office, the Office of Legal Counsel, the Solicitor General's Office, certain divisions of the Department of Justice, the Policy Planning Offices of the Federal Communications commission or Federal Trade Commissions, and the Securities and Exchange Commission, are all good examples—particularly if the job is related to your area of specialization. For instance, if you plan to specialize in telecommunications law, a few years of working for the FCC could be a tremendous asset.

Fellowships
Erin O'Hara, *Vanderbilt University Law School*

One thing that can improve your chances for an academic job is a legal fellowship at some point between your clerkship and your first attempt at the job market. Although a fellowship is not a "must have" in the same way as a circuit court clerkship, a fellowship can help in a number of ways, not the least of which is the credential itself.

Simply put, a legal fellowship can allow you to affiliate yourself with a law school and to spend your time teaching, pursuing advanced coursework, and doing research and writing. Fellowships come in several different forms. Some, such as the University of Chicago's Bigelow Fellowships, entail at least part-time teaching in the legal writing program. Others, such as the Morris Fellowships at Columbia, support work toward an advanced law degree. Still others (usually from sources outside the law schools themselves, such as the Federalist Society's John M. Olin Fellowships) simply allow law graduates to be in residence at a law school for a year to concentrate on research and writing.

A legal fellowship of any sort offers three main benefits. First, it will give you the time you need to write one or more law review articles. Remember, you should try to have at least two publications to your credit (one student note and at least one article) when you enter the job market. If you were unable to write an article during your clerkship or while you worked for a law firm, this is an excellent chance to catch up. With an increasing number of job candidates with PhD degrees and an increasing number of fellowship opportunities available to aspiring legal academics, law schools are less willing than they used to be to hire candidates without strong scholarship records. Three or more articles, if of high quality, will place you in an even better position to find a job. A fellowship that allows more time for your research and writing should in general be preferred to one that provides less flexibility.

The second important benefit, if you take a fellowship just prior to entering the market, is that it puts you back into an academic frame of mind. The world of legal practice and the world of legal academia can be very different, even in terms of the thinking you need to do. While working at a law firm, you will most likely be too busy to keep up with the hot topics being discussed in the top law reviews. Moreover, it's easy to get so engrossed in the "trees" of practice that you temporarily lose sight of the legal "forest." Making the transition from advocate to analyst isn't always easy, but having a relatively low-stress year to immerse yourself in your research and writing (and maybe some teaching) is a good way to ease your way back in.

Finally, in the case of teaching fellowships, you will end up with a set of teaching evaluations (positive, one hopes!) that will indicate to potential academic employers that you wouldn't be a disaster in front of a classroom. For the elite institutions, this is less of a factor—it's your research, not your teaching, that matters in these cases—but most lesser-ranked law schools make an effort to find faculty who take teaching seriously and who are good at it.

There are several sources for legal fellowships, and opportunities seem to increase each year. Most fellowships are sponsored by law schools and require that you remain in residence there. As of this writing, most of the top 20 schools offer one or more fellowship programs, and several schools outside of the top 20 also have fellowship opportunities. In most cases, you should take a fellowship with the highest-ranked school possible. However, some other fellowships are more portable, sponsored by philanthropic foundations that allow you to choose where you will base yourself (perhaps from a list of approved institutions). An Internet search (particularly the AALS and ABA Web sites) is also likely to turn up some solid prospects.

Advanced Law Degrees
Claire Hill, *University of Minnesota Law School*

Many law schools offer advanced law degrees, such as the LLM, and the SJD (JSD). The LLM is the law equivalent of the Master's degree and generally involves an added year of coursework. The SJD and JSD, which are the same degree (terminology is dependent on different schools), are the equivalent of a PhD in that they require a certain amount of coursework and then a dissertation.

If you have followed the traditional route thus far in your career—attended a top-ten law school, worked on law review, held a federal clerkship, published a couple of pieces, and worked two to four years for a high-prestige firm—there's little reason to pursue one of these degrees, since the credential itself is unlikely to add much to your résumé. Nevertheless, there are a few cases where the pursuit of such a degree is desirable; one such instance is if you received your JD from a middling law school. An LLM from a prestigious school may carry some of that school's cachet. If you want to develop a marketable field of specialization in which you have little or no background, a specialized LLM may help to serve that purpose.

PART 4: THE JOB MARKET

Some Observations and Predictions
Brett G. Scharffs, *Brigham Young University Law School*[5]

The job market for legal academia is consistently competitive. In 1996, for example, there were 957 candidates listed in the AALS Faculty Appointments Register, and of those, only 69 received offers—just over seven percent. Fortunately (except for those of us looking for teaching jobs that year), 1996 was the worst year for entry-level teaching positions since the Association of American Law Schools began to keep track. Since then, conditions in the job market have seen steady improvements. In 2000, only 769 applied for appointments with the AALS and of those, 115 received offers, representing a success rate of about fifteen percent. In 2003, there were 957 applicants, the same number (although hopefully not the same individuals) as in 1996. However, 143 of applicants in 2003 received offers—more than double the number who received offers in 1996.[6]

One factor that accounts for the greater numbers of faculty hired was that, at the turn of the millennium, student applications to law school were increasing and not surprisingly, there is some correlation between student demand and law school supply. But in 2006 and 2007, the number of students applying to law school was again on the decline. Nevertheless, there is reason to believe that the number of job openings will remain stable or increase due to the fact that many law schools are gradually increasing the number of faculty positions. Also, the last great boom in law school hiring

---

[5] This chapter is based upon and incorporates material from a chapter in the first edition written by Stephen M. Sheppard.
[6] AALS website, http://aals.org.cnchost.com/documents/statistics/Report_tables_0405.pdf , page 114.

took place in the 1970s; therefore, we should start to see large numbers of retirements creating more vacancies.

There have also been significant increases in the hiring of women and minority candidates throughout the past decade. In 1996, 24 women received offers in legal academia out of 293 female applicants. Successful female applicants represented 34.8% of the total number of successful applicants. Over the past decade there has been a rather steady increase in the number and percentage of women hired, with women accounting for 43.4% of the new hires in 2002 and 40.6% in 2003.[7]

In 1996, 18 of 170 minority applicants received offers. This represented a slightly higher success rate of 10.6% compared with a success rate of 8% for non-minority applicants (50 out of 624). In 2003, 21.2% of minority candidates were successful compared with 15.1% of non-minority candidates.[8]

From the perspective of job candidates, it is easy to overestimate the respective advantage or disadvantage of being male, female, or a minority. The tendency is to convince yourself that you are at a disadvantage regardless of your personal characteristics. For example, when I was on the market in 1996, I thought I was facing a nearly insurmountable obstacle because I was a white male. In my mind, law schools were in the process of trying to make up for years of failing to hire women and minorities, and the consequences, I feared, were going to fall directly on the backs of people like me.

It turns out that my concerns were largely a figment of my imagination. A recent study published in the *Journal of Legal Education* shed some light on

---

[7] AALS website, http://aals.org.cnchost.com/documents/statistics/Report_tables_0405.pdf, pages 115-116.
[8] AALS website, http://aals.org.cnchost.com/documents/statistics/Report_tables_0405.pdf, pages 117-118.

hiring trends of the past decade. It turns out that the average recent hire at the time I was looking for a teaching job was someone who looked a lot like me—a white, male graduate of Yale Law School who had been on law review, had a prestigious appellate clerkship, and had a couple of years of work experience. According to that study, most recently hired law faculty had graduated from Harvard, Yale, or another top law school. Many served as senior staff of the law review or another journal. Although most had published one or two journal articles or notes before they were hired, a substantial minority had not published at all. Most had experience in legal practice, many had completed judicial clerkships, and a sizeable minority had previous experience in law teaching. "But only the quality of the law school that they attended, whether they served on law review, and the number of years of legal practice experience significantly predicted the quality of the law school at which they were hired."[9]

If you are a year or two away from entering the teaching market, in my opinion, the most strategically useful thing you can do to give yourself a comparative advantage, by far, is to write and publish one or two law review articles before applying. One of these can serve as the basis for your job talk, which is a make-or-break element of the final leg of the hiring process—the on-campus interview. By the time many people are thinking about teaching, it is too late to choose a law school based upon its reputation for producing academics, or even to make law review or pursue a clerkship. The best way to make up for any disadvantage you may face is to demonstrate not just potential, but actual, accomplishment as a scholar. The conventional wisdom within law schools today is that the best way to pursue institutional advancement (which often means not much more than increasing the school's standing in the *U.S. News and World Report* rankings) is through faculty scholarship. Because this conventional wisdom shows no sign of subsiding, you will give yourself a substantial leg up if you are able to turn this to your comparative advantage.

---

[9] Richard E. Redding, *"Where Did You Go to Law School?" Gatekeeping For the Professoriate and its Implications for Legal Education.*, 53 J. LEGAL EDUC. 594, 605-606 (2003).

Perhaps the most unhelpful thing you can do is to send the message that you are interested in teaching because you are burned out and tired of the practice of law. It is surprising how many would-be professors submit cover letters that seem to be plaintive pleas to rescue them from the drudgery of the billable hour. To state the obvious as politely as possible, it is unlikely that you will convince a group of law professors that they should hire you because you perceive them to have a cushy sinecure that will insulate you from the need to work hard in the future.

Approaching the Job Market
Stephen J. Ware, *University of Kansas School of Law*

Once you've decided that you've built a strong enough resume, it's time to make the big leap into the job market. There will be thousands of others who have decided on the same course, but if you've followed the advice contained in this booklet so far, you should have a significant advantage over many of them.

You should approach the market along three separate tracks. The first, and undoubtedly most common, is the Association of American Law Schools. Most interviewing and hiring will proceed through the AALS via its Faculty Appointments Register and its annual Faculty Recruitment Conference, held in late October or early November. For more on the AALS process, see the next section.

The second track involves drawing on the network you've built throughout the years since you started law school. Contact the former professors with whom you've stayed in touch (you have been keeping in touch with them, haven't you?). Talk to the judge(s) for whom you clerked. Talk to other faculty members with whom you've established contact via your publications. Let them know that you are on the market and that you'd appreciate any leads they can offer, or any contacts that they might have at schools that are hiring. At the top law schools, most hiring is done on the basis of word-of-mouth, not the résumé that will appear in the AALS Register. If the chair of a hiring committee gets a call from an old friend who knows a talented candidate on the market, the chair will take this seriously—particularly if the old friend is a distinguished legal scholar.

The third track involves approaching law schools on your own. Send every law school you would even consider a cover letter along with your résumé and copies of your publications. This isn't as massive an undertaking as it may seem; there are fewer than 200 law schools, so even if you'd consider all of them, the cost of paper and postage is low enough to justify the effort. This packet will tell the schools more about you than they can learn from the AALS Register. The extra information about you, along with your personal correspondence, may catch the attention of someone who would not have noticed you in the AALS Register. To which person at the school should you address your packet? Different schools handle such applications differently, but the safest choice is to send your packet to the chair of the Faculty Appointments Committee, if you know who it is. If you don't, then you can send it to the Dean. Of course, your envelope and cover letter should be addressed to Professor Smith or Dean Jones, not "Chair, Faculty Appointments Committee."

If you are currently working and want to keep secret the fact that you're on the academic market, make that known up front. Law schools are accustomed to dealing with confidential applications. Ask interested schools to hold off on contacting your job references until late in the process—*i.e.*, at the last step, with the understanding that an offer will go through as long as the references are positive. Schools want work references primarily to make sure that you are not being forced to leave involuntarily, thus they will usually be amenable to this condition.

The AALS Process
Andrew P. Morriss, *University of Illinois College of Law*

There are two routes to becoming a law professor. One (the method by which most entry-level jobs are filled) is through the hiring process run by the AALS. The other is an ad hoc process of hiring through informal networks of faculty. There is not much we can tell you about the ad hoc networks precisely because they are ad hoc. Even if you are fortunate enough to have contacts at law schools who are able to help you get interviews through this second route, you still should participate in the AALS process. The market for entry-level law professors has very peculiar dynamics; the number of interviews you have sends a signal to the market, which in turn can significantly increase the likelihood of converting an interview into a tenure track job. In general you will be on the market during summer and fall of the year before you begin teaching, although your preparation for entering the market will have started long before you formally enter it.

THE AALS FACULTY APPOINTMENTS REGISTER

The AALS process begins with your submission of information to the AALS for inclusion in the *Faculty Appointments Register* (FAR). The *FAR* is published four times each year by the AALS, generally in late August, late September, October, and January. In 2006, the fee to list your resume in the *FAR* was $295 for the first three distributions and $330 for the fourth. Check www.aals.org for up-to-date information. From the candidates in the *FAR*, appointments committees will select candidates to invite to interviews at the AALS Faculty Recruitment Conference, sponsored by the AALS in late October or early November each year.

The *FAR* includes the resumes of candidates in a condensed, uniform format that includes information on education, work experience, sex and ethnicity, teaching and geographical preferences, bar memberships, publications, and references. Appointments committees can use the *FAR* Web site to generate lists of candidates that meet specific criteria. In addition to the short *FAR* form, candidates may also upload a full resume, which is available to appointments committees through the AALS Web site. These resumes, however, are not searchable. The hiring committee will generally not peruse these documents unless you have given them a reason to via the short *FAR* form.

To examine the characteristics of successful candidates, let's look at the *FARs* from 1998 and 1999. We can tell who got jobs in this group by comparing the names in the *FARs* with the names in the AALS Directory of Law Teachers from subsequent years. Applicants have been growing continually more qualified and so current year's numbers are likely to reflect higher qualifications.

Among all applicants, the median number of years of private practice experience was three; the median number of published law review articles was one, although over a quarter of applicants had three or more. Among those who got jobs, 72% had at least one law review article listed and 60% had two or more. By contrast, among those who did not get jobs, 44% had one or fewer law review articles. Approximately a third of the candidates had their JD from an elite law school while over half of successful candidates had this credential. More than half had an advanced degree (LLM., PhD, S.JD, or other degree)—virtually the same percentage as among successful candidates. Over half of the applicant pool and two thirds of successful candidates had some law school teaching experience, usually as an adjunct. Approximately 25% of the candidates were listed as some sort of faculty in the AALS Directory of Law Teachers in the subsequent year, although only about 16% had titles indicating full-time, tenure track appointments.

RULE 1: You must be in the first distribution of Faculty Appointments Register forms.

The first rule of a successful candidacy is that you must submit your information to the AALS before the first deadline (late July or early August). Why is this critical? Many law school appointments committees begin selecting candidates for interviews from the *FAR* almost as soon as it is available and fill most of their appointment slots before the second distribution is sent out. If you are not in the first distribution of the *FAR*, your resume will be considered only after most of the interview slots are gone and you will receive fewer interviews than if you had been in the first distribution. Approximately 50% of candidates are in the first *FAR* distribution in most years, and more than 60% of those who got jobs in the years I checked were in the first distribution—which is good news because it means you are facing serious competition from at most half the people who register with the AALS.

Because the *FAR* process is so important, you must prepare for it well in advance. Register on the AALS Web site in the spring of the year you intend to go on the market. Familiarize yourself with the information required and prepare your responses. This is not something to do at the last minute!

The information you submit to the *FAR* is what many appointments committees will look at when making a decision about whether or not to interview you. It should therefore communicate two things about you. First, you are a serious scholar with an excellent track record and the potential to produce important scholarship. Second, you will be a useful addition to the teaching faculty of the law school that hires you. Although the form is extremely limited, you can effectively communicate these things, as we will discuss below.

Although your *FAR* form will be your primary form of communication with appointments committee members, you should also be sure to upload a separate resume to the AALS Web site. The *FAR* severely limits your ability to provide details about the items on the form and a resume (in Word or Wordperfect format) gives you the chance to provide more information to the appointments committees that will be considering you.

You should ask several law professors with recent appointments committee experience and who are familiar with your record to read over your draft *FAR* form and resume before submitting them to the AALS. There are important conventions in legal academia in the use of terminology and, because the forms are so important, you should make sure that you do not inadvertently use or fail to use language that sabotages your credibility as a candidate.

Between 700 and 1,000 candidates register in the various editions of the *FAR* each year, although well over half are usually in the first distribution. Of those in the first distribution, a rough estimate is that approximately a third to half are serious candidates who will garner most of the interviews. The problem for appointments committees, therefore, is to quickly weed out the large number of non-serious candidates. At this stage, committees are usually looking for quick ways to reduce the number of resumes they have to read. Of course, you will already have taken a number of important steps to bring your candidacy to the attention of appointments committees, even before you register in the *FAR*. For at least some schools, however, this will be their first serious look at your candidacy.

RULE 2: *Don't give a committee an easy reason to not consider you.*

Among the easiest ways to handicap your candidacy is to include geographical and subject restrictions in your *FAR* form. These are very important fields because they will give appointments committees a quick way to eliminate you from consideration.

For teaching, the *FAR* asks you to list subjects you would "most like to teach," "other subjects I may be interested in teaching," and "other subjects I would be willing to teach, if asked." You can rank the top three subjects for "most like to teach" and four for the other two categories. You can also add a brief comment to each section. The most common mistake made by candidates in the teaching section is to make themselves appear to be overly narrow and uncooperative by restricting their teaching interests to niche or boutique courses.

In theory, of course, you would probably most like to teach courses that overlap with your research. Listing only highly specialized subjects that are likely to draw only a few students, however, will not make you a valued contributor to the teaching mission of a law school. Be sure to include two or three "bread and butter" courses in each of these sections. Such courses include any first year course, core upper-class courses (*e.g.* business associations, wills and trusts, federal courts, administrative law, securities regulation). Do not make comments restricting what you are willing to teach. Such restrictions will either add no new information (*e.g.* "I will teach any course except tax" when your resume includes no information that suggests you are competent to teach tax classes) or lose you a potential interview at a school that really wants someone to teach a particular subject. Do use the comment lines to signal flexibility (*e.g.* "I would like to teach a first year class"). If you have a particular specialty (international law or intellectual property, for example), you should be sure to use the teaching subjects to signal your willingness to teach a large enrollment course outside the specialty.

Why is this so important? Law school teaching is a zero sum game—someone has to teach unpopular courses (Civil Procedure, for example). The less likely you are to teach them, the more likely I am to have to do so. Moreover, if you are teaching classes that draw only 20 students a semester rather than 50, it is likely that there will be more students in my classes, increasing the number of exams and papers. Therefore, from a self-interested point of view, appointments committees will not want to hire inflexible people because doing so increases their workloads.

The geographic restriction sections include lines in which you can specify "I will only accept a position in…" and "I will not accept a position in…" These lines must be left blank, regardless of your actual preferences. There are three important reasons. First, even if you have strong reasons to think you will need to be in a specific location (a partner's job, for example), you need to get lots of interviews to help generate excitement about your candidacy. Even regions with many law schools (*e.g.* New York City) have only a small fraction of the jobs available in the country as a whole. Second, many schools in less desirable locations are well aware of the problems their location poses and have programs to solve those problems. Many law schools in small towns, for example, have spousal hiring policies that can help with two-career couples. Even if you don't think you want to live in a small rural town, if a school in such a location wants you, it will work hard to solve the problems its location creates for you. Give the school the opportunity to do so because you can always decline the offer later. Third, you don't know now what your preferences will be six months after submitting the form. If you really want to be a law professor and your only offer is from a region where you never imagined living, you may have to rethink your geographic preferences in light of your options. You should preserve your options.

Once you've submitted your AALS form, your work is not done. You cannot rely on the *FAR* to get you interviews.

RULE 3: Don't rely on the AALS process to get interviews.

Your job is to get yourself noticed by as many law school appointments committees as possible. Unless you get noticed, no one will be reading your *FAR* form or downloading your resume. You can do two important things to improve your chances of being noticed.

- Write to the appointments committees at schools in which you have an interest. If you don't know who the appointments chair is, call the school's dean's office and find out. (A letter addressed "To Whom It May Concern" signals a lack of interest on your part.) Enclose a resume and briefly make a case why you would be a good fit for the school by demonstrating that you have examined the school's job posting in the AALS's *Placement Bulletin*, to which you receive an online subscription as part of the *FAR* registration, and the school's web site for information about its program.

- Mobilize your network of references to make phone calls and write letters on your behalf. As an appointments committee chair, I've gotten calls from the heads of federal agencies and famous faculty at top schools, all eager to tout the merits of a candidate. This is an excellent way to get on a committee's agenda.

Once the *FAR* is distributed, you will start to receive calls from appointments committees seeking to schedule interviews with you at the Faculty Recruitment Conference (FRC).

The AALS Faculty Recruitment Conference
Andrew Morriss, *University of Illinois College of Law*

The FRC is held each year at a large hotel in Washington, D.C., or Chicago. The conference begins Thursday afternoon with registration, a reception, and some information sessions. Schools schedule twenty to thirty half-hour interviews during Friday and Saturday, from which they select a smaller number of candidates to invite back to campus for a full interview. You will have to pay to attend the conference yourself. Be sure to register early so that you can stay at the conference hotel as this will make getting to your interviews much easier. Of course, dress conservatively and professionally.

When scheduling interviews, keep in mind that the interviews are not scheduled with time between them for you to get to your next interview and that the hotels where the conference is held are very large. You will have to control your schedule to ensure you have time to get from one interview to the next. Particularly if the FRC is held in Washington, where the hotel has three separate towers, you may have to travel a significant distance between interviews. (Take this into account when choosing shoes to wear to the interview.) Allowing a half hour between interviews is therefore desirable, as it will enable you to arrive at your next interview on time and without being out of breath from running. Walking your interview schedule the day before will also help you avoid being late.

Most schools fill their Friday interview slots first, so when a school calls to offer you an interview at the FRC, try to get a Friday interview to preserve the Saturday slots for schools that will call you later. Moreover, the interview process is even worse for the appointments committees than it is for you. True, they have jobs already, but they generally do not get a break between interviews at all. By the end of the day, most are tired of the entire process and by the end of Saturday, are considering how long it will take them to get a cab to the airport. An interview at 3 p.m. on Saturday is better than no interview, but it isn't as good as one at 9 a.m. on Friday.

If you are a particularly desirable candidate, you may receive and accept offers of interviews at the beginning of the process and later get a better offer for a particular time slot. If you lose interest in a school, it is perfectly acceptable to cancel the interview, particularly if you give the school sufficient notice so that they will be able to fill the slot with someone else. Under no circumstances is it acceptable to cancel an interview by leaving a note at the AALS message center or by simply not showing up. Always personally contact the appointments committee chair and explain that you received many more interview requests than you can accommodate and so you must regretfully cancel your interview. Appointments committees from various schools often share information and if you behave rudely toward one, word will get around to the others.

Your half-hour slot is your only chance to sell yourself to the appointments committee. Your goal is to secure a call-back interview. Everything else is secondary because without a callback, you won't be getting a faculty position. To maximize your chances of a callback, there are some simple things you must do. Be on time. When your time slot arrives, knock firmly on the door to let the committee know you are there. Don't let your good manners inhibit the firmness of your knock—if the interview ahead of you is running over, that person is taking your time. Don't waste time in the interview eating, even if offered food.

There are also some important substantive tips for preparing for the interview. First, you should moot the interview beforehand with faculty mentors. This is an excellent way to hone your answers for the real thing. Second, you should do some research on the schools you will be seeing. Third, you should spend time preparing answers on teaching and scholarship, the two most important areas about which you will be questioned.

RULE 4: Know who is interviewing you.

You should learn enough about each school with which you will interview to impress the appointments committee members with your seriousness about wanting a job at their school. This means you should carefully examine the school's Web site, looking for information about what the school considers its strengths and who are the most active faculty members. Look on SSRN to see if there are working papers posted from the school. Google the school and check some of the applicant bulletin boards. And, be sure to check The Leiter Law School Reports (http://leiterlawschool.typepad.com/) on the top forty or so law schools, Larry Solum's Legal Theory blog (http://lsolum.blogspot.com/) on entry-level hirings, and Dan Filler's blog, Concurring Opinion (http://www.concurringopinions.com/), on lateral hirings. These will give you important information about schools' hiring strategies in the past and turnover.

To research the interview team you will meet, talk to the appointments committee member who calls you to arrange the interview. Ask which committee members will be at the interview, and learn more about those faculty members. Check their publications on Westlaw or Lexis and at least skim several. Google the committee members to see if any have blogs. Read the most recent few years of *U.S. News & World Report* law school rankings and look for trends in the rankings. (*U.S. News* is a controversial measure of "quality," but it is a measure that reports useful data on the schools it ranks.) All of this can give you important clues about the committee and about how to respond to questions you will be asked. Are the most active scholars on the appointments committee? Do members of the committee have a particular agenda that their publications reveal? Make careful notes so you can remind yourself before entering the interview.

RULE 5: *Have answers ready for obvious questions.*

You will be asked about your scholarship plans and your teaching interests. You must have answers ready for these questions.

Regarding scholarship, the questions are all aimed at determining two things: (1) Do you have an agenda for your scholarship, or are you a dilettante who skips from project to project? (2) Will you be someone who will regularly write because you love to write or are you someone who will struggle to produce scholarship?

The answer to the research agenda question must be that you have given a great deal of thought to what you want to write over the next three to five years and have definite ideas about how to structure those articles. Your answer to a question about your plans for your next article cannot be, "I think contracts sounds interesting." Rather, it should connect your next piece to your previous work. For example, if your first article was on interpreting form contracts in consumer relationships and your next piece will examine employment contracts, answer the question by saying, "My first article was on form contracts in the consumer context. That got me interested in the more general problem of contracts where there is little real bargaining and so I plan to write about interpretation of employment contracts in circumstances where the employee is given a take-it-or-leave-it offer to see if the same principles can be applied." Be ready to explain the connection further if asked.

On teaching, you should come to the interview prepared to talk about how you plan to teach the courses you listed on your *FAR* as the ones you are most interested in teaching. Go to a university law library and look over the casebooks available for those courses. Talk to your favorite professors about which books they have used and why they chose the books they did. Think over your law school career and compare the different teaching techniques you observed. Then, instead of responding, "Oh, I think I'll use the Socratic method in Property," you can be ready to say, "In law school, my property class used the Singer casebook but I think I would prefer to start with the Dukeminier and Krier casebook because I like the way it mixes law and economics analysis with legal history." Don't just memorize a casebook name or two—you may be asked follow up questions and you will just look foolish if you can't back up your initial statement. Another key teaching point is being able to describe how your background makes you well suited to teaching a particular subject area (*e.g.* practice experience in a particular area).

Questions about teaching are also your chance to signal your willingness to be a good citizen. When asked about the courses you listed, be sure to convey that while you hope to be able to teach Property, you are most eager to teach a first year class and are willing to meet the school's needs. It is important to show a willingness to teach classes outside your area of expertise if called upon to do so. It may even be worth mentioning that this would be an opportunity to learn a new subject, as there is almost no better way to learn a subject than to have to teach it.

You will also be asked about why you want to be a law professor. Your answer to this question should signal your eagerness to become a serious scholar. Good answers do not involve lists of what you did not like about practice or desires for life of leisure. You want to be a law professor because you care passionately about making a contribution to legal scholarship and teaching students. It is a positive career choice, not a choice driven by your lack of satisfaction with prior career choices.

RULE 6: *Be enthusiastic about the school.*

The people interviewing you work at the school they represent. Most of them, and possibly all if the committee is well-chosen, like working at that school. They want to hire other people who will be happy working at their school—if they don't, they will be back at the AALS in a few years looking for a replacement. Your job in the interview is to convey your enthusiasm for working at their school. You might prefer to work at a top ten school in New York City, but when you are interviewing with a second tier school in a rural location, you need to be enthusiastic about the school you are interviewing with, rather than another school.

Being enthusiastic about a school means knowing something about where the school is located and what the community is like. Don't ask, as a candidate once did when I was on the Case Western Reserve University School of Law appointments committee, "So where exactly is Cleveland? It's in Ohio, right?" Instead, be ready with a question that shows real interest in the community. The FRC interview is not a place to waste time getting information about the school—you can do that during the callback process. Thus, your questions about the school should be ones designed to signal things about you, rather than to gain information. Ask about support for scholarship, faculty culture, whether there are regular workshop series, and the like. These questions signal that you are a serious scholar. You can find out what winters are like or whether there is a good retirement plan later.

If the interview threatens to run over and you have another interview immediately after the current one, you will have to make a choice about whether or not to run late for the next interview or not. Know in advance the relative importance of each school to your job search. If you need to leave, politely explain that you have another interview but would be delighted to continue the conversation later. If you are delayed, call the other interview room as soon as you leave to explain that your prior interview ran late and that you are hurrying to the next one.

As your half-hour draws to a close, be sure to thank the interviewers for their time and express renewed interest in the position. They may explain how their search will proceed; if they do not, it is perfectly acceptable to ask what the next steps will be. Some schools will decide at the end of the FRC who to invite back, others must return to their faculties with a proposed list of callbacks. Some committees may ask for contact information during the conference, and may later invite you for a meal or drink. Be sure to regularly check your cell phone, room phone, and the AALS message center for messages to make sure you promptly respond to such offers.

RULE 7: Follow up.

After the interview, write a brief, sincere note to the appointments committee chair, thanking the committee for its time and reiterating your interest in the position. Make a brief reference to something you discussed in the interview, if possible (*e.g.* "I am particularly excited about learning more about your new international law center"). Do this immediately—committees often meet at the end of the conference or the first day home to make offers. Your note will signal that you are interested and will be a good colleague.

If you get a callback, congratulations. If you don't, consider calling some of the schools after a decent interval and asking the committee chair to point out any weaknesses in your interview. You might learn something useful for the on-campus visits at the schools that do call you back.

Compared to ten years ago, or even five years ago, there is a wealth of advice (some good, some not so good) available online. A good starting place is Cornell Law Prof. Bradley Wendel's Web site "The Big Rock Candy Mountain: How to Get a Job in Law Teaching," (http://www.lawschool.cornell.edu/faculty-pages/wendel/teaching.htm), which not only includes his advice, but also links to lots of other people's advice as well.

There are two more topics that you need to consider: faculty politics and affirmative action. Politics always plays a role in hiring decisions. The only question is how it will do so. Some faculty politics is surprisingly petty: if Professor Smith knocked off Professor Jones' favorite candidate last year,

Professor Jones might try to return the favor this year. Sometimes politics is simply ideology, sometimes it is personal. In either case, it has nothing to do with you. The only thing you can do about it is to minimize the chances that you will be viewed as an ideologue rather than a scholar. When describing your research agenda, it is probably advisable to avoid ideologically charged subjects. There is no benefit in giving a member of the committee a reason to oppose you on political grounds. Having a sense of humor, particularly about yourself and your politics, and choosing your paper topics carefully can also go a long way toward insulating you from political objections.

The same is true of affirmative action. Law schools are under intense pressure from the ABA and the AALS to improve their diversity in every sense but political diversity. There is nothing you can do about this and so you shouldn't let it worry you. You should not, however, under any circumstances, attempt to manipulate the AALS forms to gain "credit" for being in a favored group. The *FAR* asks you for your race and gender. Answer honestly and be sure to answer, since a failure to respond to these questions is often read as an anti-affirmative action statement. Because most existing law faculty approve of affirmative action, mischaracterizing yourself or failing to respond will be read as a negative.

Common Meat Market Questions
Compiled by David E. Bernstein, *George Mason University School of Law*

1. Why do you want to be a law professor?
2. Why do you want to teach?
3. What kind of public service activities are you interested in, at the law school and in general?
4. If invited to give a job talk at our law school, what would you talk about?
5. What would your ideal course load for a year be? (Or, name the four classes you would most like to teach.)
6. What are your future research plans?
7. How do you enjoy law practice?

8. How would you teach [whatever subject you listed on your AALS form]?
9. What are you looking for in a law school?
10. Why would someone like you from [your law school] want to teach at [our law school]?
11. What can we tell you about our law school and community?
12. Where do you see yourself in ten years?
13. What was your favorite class (or professor) in law school and why?
14. What are your personal interests and hobbies?

The Campus Visit
Brett G. Scharffs, *Brigham Young University Law School* [10]

Soon after the meat market, hiring committees will decide which of the candidates they interviewed at the AALS to invite for a visit to the campus. If you get such a call, then congratulations are in order. You've gone from being a lone face in a crowd of hundreds to a contender in a much narrower field of competitors; it's costly to invite candidates to campus, so in most cases, law schools won't invite more than three or four people. Indeed, at times, only one candidate is invited in the hope that further invitations will be unnecessary. If the number of candidates who will advance to this stage was not made clear to you during the AALS interview, the phone call inviting you for the visit is the proper time to ask.

Campus visits will vary somewhat from place to place but generally last a day to a day-and-a-half. They will include a campus tour, including a visit to the library, a series of interviews with faculty and usually students, one or two meals with faculty, and a meeting with the dean at the end of your visit. In most cases, the centerpiece of your visit will be the so-called job talk. Although the job talk takes a variety of forms, it usually consists of a

---

[10] Much of this chapter is based upon John Moser's chapter on the same subject in the first edition.

presentation to the faculty of twenty to thirty minutes on a current research project, outlining the basic contours of your research, and another thirty to forty minutes of questions.

It is imperative that you be ready to accept an invitation for a campus visit when it is extended; if you have delayed getting serious about your job talk until this point, you have put yourself in a very bad position. Ideally, your job talk should be based upon an article that is almost ready to be submitted to law reviews for publication. It should be largely finished before you go to AALS, because one of the questions you should expect to be asked is what your current research agenda is and what you would talk about if you are invited for an on-campus visit. No one on the hiring committee wants to look like an idiot for inviting a candidate who is likely to belly flop on the job talk.

Because the job talk is so important, a bit more about how to set yourself up for success is warranted. First, your choice of topics is critical. It should flow naturally from your past scholarly work, indicating that you think in terms of a larger research agenda. It should also be somewhat broad—remember that most of your audience will not share the same specialization as you—as well as provocative, timely, and perhaps even controversial. The topic should be accessible enough to draw in non-specialists but not so general that it appears overly ambitious or vague. You must have a thesis that you can state clearly and defend. You must have a familiarity with existing literature and a sense of where your argument fits. You must marshal evidence, anticipate objections, and be prepared to respond to them. One of the best pieces of advice I received as a rookie professor came from a distinguished senior colleague who told me to look for an interesting debate taking place within an area I found interesting and to insert myself into the middle of it. He recommended that I think of the major participants in that debate as my primary audience. In my view, this was very good advice.

Another of my colleagues insists that the difference between a successful and unsuccessful job talk can be summarized in one word: *insight*. A presentation is successful, he says, if it forces you to think about a subject in a different way. Providing genuine insight may be too tall an order, and all of us often fall short of this objective, but I think it does describe what we should be aiming for in a setting of this type.

Your audience will be making a number of judgments about you based upon your performance in the job talk. First, does the candidate have scholarly chops? Here they are making an assessment about whether you are someone who will likely be able to have success researching and writing in the law. Second, is this someone who will be able to hold their own in the classroom? Although there are a wide variety of teaching styles that work in law school, the ability to think on one's feet, to listen and respond to questions and challenges, and to explain oneself clearly are vital skills of a law professor. Third, is this someone who I can stand to have at faculty meetings? You will be judged on whether you are fair-minded, willing to listen to and understand opposing points of view, and simply whether it would be painful to have you in the building. Focusing on these generalities does not provide a formula for crafting your job talk or handling questions, but it is helpful to understand what your audience is thinking about.

Once you've put together your talk, practice it often, alone in front of a mirror and with anyone who will listen. Find out in advance how long your talk should run, and plan accordingly—if your practice runs take you beyond that length of time, go back and make some cuts. Speaking longer than asked is a sure way to annoy your audience.

Also, give some thought to the sort of questions that your talk is likely to generate. Often faculty will go to great lengths to find objections to your argument. Don't take this personally; it is an established academic tradition, and they want to see how you handle yourself in the face of apparently hostile questioning. This means, however, that you need to go into it prepared to offer satisfactory responses. In fact, it's a good idea to leave some issues in your talk intentionally open-ended, as long as you have them worked out in your mind. That way, you can (to some extent) anticipate what will be asked and be ready with an answer, although it's better not to make it obvious that you were expecting the question. Of course, you never really know what questions will be thrown at you, and it is entirely possible that you will be asked something that you can't answer. In that case, it is acceptable to admit that you hadn't considered the question before, but be sure to say that it is a good question and one that you will think about. Try not to say this three times in a row.

One final note regarding your presentation: if you are speaking on a topic that someone on the faculty has written about, make sure to read the article in advance and mention it during your talk. It certainly pays for you to be able to say, "I agree with almost everything in Professor Jones's wonderful article. One minor disagreement, however...." As for the interviews you will have during your visit, much of the advice given in the section on AALS interviews applies here. You will want to demonstrate above all that you are a competent and creative thinker, but at the same time, a personable colleague. There is one major difference between the interviews at this stage and those that take place at the AALS. In the earlier situation, you had only a half-hour to convince the hiring committee of your merits. That means the focus had to remain on you and your qualifications. The on-campus interviews will be a bit more relaxed and most of those interviewing you will already know quite a bit about you by this point.

Therefore, you should take the opportunity to learn more about *them*. By now, you should be familiar with the writings of most of the faculty. In your meetings with them, probe them about their work. Ask how they incorporate their scholarship into their teaching. In most cases, the final hiring decision will have to be unanimous or nearly so. Thus, at this stage, you will be looking to find as many allies as you can while avoiding making enemies who will block your candidacy.

Similar advice applies if you have a chance to meet with students. Although it is unlikely that students will have a formal voice in the hiring process, it is not uncommon for the committee to ask students for their input. When you meet with them, don't let the whole conversation focus on you. Ask the students about their future plans; if any of them have scholarly aspirations of their own, talk to them about their work. Also, ask them about the school's strengths and weaknesses. And it doesn't hurt to be able to talk about your teaching methods in a way that will win their approval. For example, mention that you hold regular brown-bag lunches to get to know the students informally or that you always make a point of holding review sessions.

You can be expected to be asked about your teaching interests. A couple of obvious pointers apply. First, you should try to find out what the school's curricular needs and priorities are. There may be some differences of view within the faculty on this subject. If there is someone you know on the faculty, or with whom you have developed some rapport, you may be able to gather useful information. Second, it is a good idea to be, and sound, somewhat flexible. Of course, you can't simply express an eagerness to teach any subject, but it is a good idea to convey an attitude of open-mindedness. Law professors are often asked to cover a course that is not their preference; it is a good idea to communicate a constructive attitude in this regard.

Finally, remember to treat the nonacademic staff with respect. The school's secretaries will not be directly involved in the hiring decision, but they may be asked about you. And if you behaved in a demanding, arrogant, or ungrateful manner toward them, they will remember. Law faculties do not want to hire jerks, no matter how impressive their résumés.

While it is not unheard of to receive a formal offer on the spot, in most cases, you will not hear back for some time after the campus visit. Upon your return home, it is good form to write thank you notes to those with whom you spent the most time. It is also wise to contact those who have been supporting your candidacy to let them know exactly where things stand. Schools care a great deal about how other schools are responding to you, and your supporters can help make sure that good news travels fast. "Joe has an interview at Vanderbilt—Emily really impressed Illinois." After your interview some of your supporters may well be making crucial calls (indeed, you should ask them to), and they need to know the current situation.

Aside from these efforts, however, there is nothing to do but wait and hope for good news. If you were the first among several to visit the campus, it may be a few weeks before you hear anything. Generally, hiring committees will decide on two or three candidates, ranked in order of preference, and will then make an offer to the first on the list. If their first choice turns down the offer, they will go to the next on the list. The waiting game can be excruciating.

If you receive an offer, now is the time to discuss salary, summer research support, relocation expenses, and course load and subjects. You may feel some pressure to give a quick response, since schools will not want to lose out on their next-choice candidates while waiting for you to make up your mind. On the other hand, it is generally viewed as poor form to force a candidate to give an answer when you are waiting to hear back from other schools with which you have interviewed. Common sense and good faith are the watchwords here.

If you do not receive an offer, remember to be gracious. We often learn more about people from how they act in the face of disappointment than how they act in the face of triumph. Thank you notes and acknowledgments may be appropriate. A measure of perspective is also useful. The best candidate is not always selected. Sometimes there are compromises. Sometimes it turns out not to be possible to hire that year after all. Sometimes the faculty gets excited about a lateral hire. Sometimes there are issues of curricular fit, diversity, or simple personality that tip the scales. It is often possible to find out what your perceived strengths and weaknesses were, especially if you listen carefully and give the person on the other end of the line an opportunity to open up. In this process it is important to have thick skin. If being a law professor is what you really want, it is also important to be a little bit tenacious. Given that many schools are not interviewing for teachers in a curricular area in any particular year, it is often the case that you will have more success the second time around, especially if you have used the intervening year to publish an article or two.

Public Interest Litigation as a Career
Scott Bullock, *Institute for Justice*

The scene: a hot Mississippi evening in June inside an African-American church.

The people: local parishioners; a civil rights activist who was Jesse Jackson's state campaign manager in the 1980s; Martin Luther King III, the son of the storied civil rights leader; the Archie family of Canton, Mississippi; and three non-religious, libertarian lawyers from Washington, D.C.

The event: a prayer vigil the night before a court hearing that will decide whether the State of Mississippi can use eminent domain not for a public use but to take the land and homes of the Archie family to give it to Nissan to build an automobile plant.

After several talks, prayers, and hymns, my colleagues and I joined hands with the Archies, the parishioners, Mr. King, and others and sang the civil rights anthem: "We Shall Overcome." It was what we at the Institute for Justice call an "IJ moment," a perfect capturing in time of what we are fighting for and what public interest law is all about. I will also never forget the day when I was able to call Andrew Archie, the patriarch of the Archie family, to tell him that he and his family could stay on the land they had owned since the 1940s—the first land the family had ever owned.

Lawyers in private practice are hired guns. They do what the client wants within the bounds of broad ethical rules. In public interest law, a lawyer has both a client *and* a cause. In Mississippi, we represented the Archie family and our cause was to end eminent domain abuse within the state. In public interest law, you can pick the causes and cases you wish to champion. A public interest lawyer seeks to use litigation and all related means to represent the interests of a client and a cause to shape jurisprudence.

The Institute for Justice is an avowedly classical liberal organization. But there are public interest organizations across the ideological spectrum. Remember, all that public interest law means is that you have a client and a cause. So Pat Robertson and Ralph Nader can both rightly claim that they run public interest legal organizations.

Public interest law is distinct from what is often referred to as "legal services." The aim of legal services is to provide legal assistance to those who cannot afford it. With public interest law, your goal, in addition to providing zealous representation to your clients, is to change the world.

To be successful in public interest law, you must reorientate your way of thinking, even in law school, away from the normal practice of law (or what we sometimes refer to as "boring law").

Many would-be law students write us asking what law school is the best one for people with classical liberal ideas. Both George Mason and University of Chicago have reputations for taking a more libertarian approach, but there are so many factors in deciding where to go to school that ideological leanings are not the most important consideration. On one hand, it is usually a good idea to go to the best school that you get into. On the other hand, it may not be worth incurring huge amounts of debt in order to go to a school that is only slightly better than a less expensive university (or a school for which you have a scholarship). If you have tens of thousands of dollars of student loans, you may feel you have to work at a firm in order to pay them off. A few private schools do have loan forgiveness for public interest lawyers, and this is something that you can look into when applying.

Of course, to prepare yourself for a full-time or side career in public interest law, you should do as well as you possibly can in law school. You should take as many constitutional law and related courses as you can. You should also seek out classes or clinics that give you hands-on legal experience through such things as representation of clients under the supervision of a lawyer and moot courts.

Although you should try your best to get good grades, there is no substitute for actually getting involved in public interest law as early as possible in law school, thereby introducing yourself to a public interest organization (and they to you). You should do a clerkship with an organization that attracts your interest. While there, you should demonstrate your dedication to the cause and your ability to produce results in a very time-sensitive manner. (Litigation is driven by often inflexible deadlines. There is no time to endlessly ponder legal questions!) Most organizations, including our own, now hire new lawyers that have done clerkships for our group and have a proven track record. The good news is that many law schools now have public interest law programs that fund—in full or partially—summer clerkships for law students, especially after the first year. Indeed, most of our summer clerks come from one of these programs (or from the outstanding IHS Koch Summer Fellows Program of the Charles G. Koch Foundation). Apply to one of these programs, get accepted, and come to work for the Institute or another public interest group. If you don't get the fellowship, try to figure out a way to make a clerkship happen even if it could be a financial struggle to do so. (The Institute and many other groups only have a limited supply of paid clerkships.)

While in law school, you should apply for the seminar on public interest law that the Institute for Justice holds every year in July. It is a three-day-long weekend packed with both theory and practice and provides an excellent starting point for a career in public interest law or the ability to do public interest cases on a pro bono basis while you are in private practice.

Once you have worked for a particular group, stay in touch with the organization throughout law school. Tell them you would like to work there upon graduation. You have to be flexible when it comes to job opportunities. Most public interest groups are not locked into a tight and routine hiring schedule like large law firms.

Before going to work at a public interest group, you should consider doing a clerkship with a judge. Most people find their clerkship experiences to be very worthwhile. With clerkships, you can see the nuts and bolts of actual litigation. Students often overlook the possibility of clerking for state court judges, but state courts have some of the most interesting and cutting-edge constitutional litigation. Consider a state supreme court as a possible alternative to a federal court clerkship. It you want to go into private practice for a while, try to go to a firm where you will receive the most amount of litigation experience, even if it is at a small or medium-sized firm. Many associates at large firms are stuck in "document production" for years, without ever taking a deposition, let alone appearing in court.

Even if you cannot make public interest law a full-time career, there will be opportunities for you to take on public interest cases while you are in private practice. Toward that end, there are important lessons to keep in mind whether you are practicing public interest law full or part time. Among these are the following:

In public interest law, you must be entrepreneurial. You can't wait for cases to walk in the door. You have to go out, make things happen, and find great cases. Moreover, there are no "form books" for public interest law. Lawyers in private practice often consult books and online sources and take a very cautious approach to the arguments they make and the strategies they deploy. In public interest law, you have to be comfortable creating legal arguments and strategies that perhaps have not been tested in the past—and still be able to sleep at night!

In addition to litigating your cases in court, you must also try your cases in the court of public opinion. Most lawyers typically refuse to speak to the media and rarely let their clients do so. You have to speak in English, not legalese, and explain your case and your client's cause to the public, and let your client do the same thing. You have to put a human face on the cause you seek to advance, and that face is the client's. You have to capture the rhetoric of the public debate to be successful.

You should also form non-traditional alliances and work with people and organizations of many different backgrounds and interests. You should not have ideological litmus tests for potential supporters. If a group agrees with you on a particular issue (and so long as they are not a racist or another type of disreputable organization), you should work with them on an issue. It can be a powerful statement to stand with someone and state that even though the two of you agree on very little, on this issue, you have joined forces because what the government is doing is so wrong. Once you have established a relationship with them, you may very well have the chance to speak with them about the larger freedom philosophy and perhaps influence their thinking.

An integral part of public interest law is grassroots activism. You have to become adept at organizing and participating in rallies, demonstrations, vigils, etc. I have spent many an evening on the back of a pick-up truck with a bullhorn. If you think that that is not the proper role of a lawyer, then you might want to re-think getting involved in public interest law.

To succeed in public interest law, you must be "real world." You will be litigating very important and cutting-edge constitutional theories, but you will also be counseling, and sometimes comforting, clients, dealing with mundane disputes about standing, ripeness, and abstention doctrines, and touring neighborhoods and buildings. At times, you may have to go into dangerous and completely unfamiliar territory to meet with potential clients. (The clients don't come to you, You must go to the clients!) You also have to be able to relate to and communicate with people from many different backgrounds and beliefs. You have to be caring, likeable, and believable if someone is going to entrust his case to you and your organization. Public interest law requires combining a number of different skills. If just thinking and blogging about legal issues is your primary interest, public interest law is not for you. If you only like to go out and network and meet people and not engage in serious research and writing into the Constitution, public interest is not for you. One of my favorite writers, Albert Murray, said that one of the most effective types of people is a "down-home intellectual," which is essentially what you have to be to succeed in public interest law.

As a public interest lawyer, it is always important to be principled. Take on cases because you believe in the issue and want passionately to vindicate the cause. Don't be political. Don't get involved in cases on behalf of political candidates or cases that are tied simply to the interests of a particular political party. You will inevitably be disappointed, and most often you will end up compromising your principles. In addition to not being political, you should also not do the bidding of a particular private business. If a business asks you to do a case, it may very well not be for principled reasons but rather so that the business can limit competition. Unfortunately, many established businesses do not support free competition and private property rights. There is a world of difference between being pro-free market and pro-business, and you must always be on the side of markets and the protection of property rights.

While always being principled, it is also very important to be practical. The law usually changes incrementally. Never compromise your principles, but you also have to recognize that the law is probably not going to change overnight. Think of litigating cases where you can significantly advance the ball on a particular issue even if you will not be able to take it as far you might think it should go.

As a public interest lawyer, you must also be resilient. Because you will be trying to change the law and the world, there will be setbacks and losses along the way, no matter how well you present your arguments and how poorly the government does in defending its unjust laws. A local jazz musician friend of mine, Randal Carter-El, had a favorite saying that was printed on the cards at his memorial service: "The greatest test of courage on Earth is to face defeat without losing heart." As a public interest lawyer, you have to adopt that saying. And, sometimes, out of a loss, can come great things. The experience of litigating the *Kelo v. City of New London* case is a great example of that. The loss at the Supreme Court has led to an incredible backlash against eminent domain abuse among the public, legislatures, and other courts. You can lose a battle but end up winning the war.

Public interest law involves litigation, which means that you have to be aggressive. That can mean, at times, arguing and fighting with other lawyers. Since those lawyers typically represent government oppression, you might think it would not be a difficult thing for classical liberal lawyers to do. But argument and confrontation can cause a great degree of stress in many people, even if they believe passionately in what they seek to vindicate. Some people who are very smart and committed have found that litigation is just not something they can do. Think about whether your personality matches the demands of litigation. You have to stand your ground and occasionally confront the opposing side or the bad guys will definitely take advantage of you and your clients.

Despite the need to need to be firm in your dealings with the other side, it is vitally important, however, that you be a happy warrior in the cause of freedom. Too many litigators cannot turn off the need to be aggressive with opposing counsel and instead adopt a boorish personality with others in their life. It is always important to be open and optimistic, and to infuse your way of dealing with others with a polite and sunny approach. Not only will the ideas and causes you seek to advance be more appealing, you will also lead a happier life. No question that righteous anger has its place, but a positive and open approach will inevitably lead to broader (and more joyous!) results.

One of the great things about being a lawyer is that you have the ability to fight abuses of individual rights head-on and to make a real-world impact. You have the ability to be a champion of the Constitution. And the Constitution needs both individuals who will take a stand for their rights and skilled advocates who will represent those individuals in court. If those two groups of people do not exist, then the Constitution largely consists of just words on an old piece of paper. That is why public interest litigation in the advancement of individual liberty is so important, and so fun.

Appendix I: LEGAL ACADEMIC CAREER BIBLIOGRAPHY AND USEFUL WEB SITES

Compiled by Elaine Hawley, *Institute for Humane Studies*

ACADEMIC LAW CAREER

- "The Big Rock Candy Mountain: How to Get a Job in Law Teaching," by Brad Wendel. June 30, 2006.

    http://ww3.lawschool.cornell.edu/faculty-pages/wendel/teaching.htm

- *Breaking Into the Academy: the 2002-2004 Michigan Journal of Race & Law Guide for Aspiring Law Professors*, edited by Gabriel J. Chin & Denise C. Morgan.

    http://students.law.umich.edu/mjrl/guide/Guide.pdf

    This special edition is updated every few years. Although nominally oriented towards minority candidates, the guide expands on the AALS article - "Uncloaking Law School Hiring."

- *Bringing Justice to the People: The Story of the Freedom—Based Public Law Movement*, by Lee Edwards. Heritage Books, 2004.

    For history and information on conservative and libertarian public interest law.

- "Careers in Law Teaching," by Eric Goldman. Updated Feb 2007.

    http://www.ericgoldman.org/Resources/becomingalawprofessor.htm

    This Web site is a goldmine of information and links, providing resources and advice for becoming a law professor (specifically for getting a job as a full-time tenure-track professor at a law school).

- "Information and Advice for Persons Interested in Teaching Law," prepared by Brian Leiter "with input from many colleagues over the years." September 2000.

    http://www.utexas.edu/law/faculty/bleiter/GUIDE.HTM

- "Matchmaker, Matchmaker, Make Me a Match: An Insider's Guide to the Faculty Hiring Process" by Debra R Cohen. September 21, 2006. Available with free login at SSRN: http://ssrn.com/abstract=931995

- "Uncloaking Law School Hiring: A Recruit's Guide to the AALS Faculty Recruitment Conference." AALS

  http://www.aals.org/frs/jle.html

  Although published in the *Journal of Legal Education* in 1988, much of the advice is still pertinent, and reputedly, this article remains the seminal piece on the AALS process.

LAW CLERKSHIPS

- *Behind the Bench: The Guide to Judicial Clerkships,* by Debra M. Strauss. *Gilberts Law Summaries*, 2002.

  http://www.judicialclerkships.com/book.htm

  "Strauss demystifies the clerkship process. Drawing from the experiences of clerks and judges, she explains all aspects of clerkships—what clerkships are, what kind of work clerks do, why you should apply, how to find and apply for the type of clerkship that would be right for you, how to give a strong interview, and why clerkships give you stellar credentials that prospective employers will actively seek out."

- Courting Clerkships: The NALP Judicial Clerkship Study. NALP/ABA 2000.

  http://www.nalp.org/content/index.php?pid=135

- Federal Judges Law Clerk Hiring Plan

  http://www.cadc.uscourts.gov/internet/lawclerk.nsf/Home?OpenForm

  This is the comprehensive site for the clerking application process, with information, critical dates, FAQs, links to application etc. Annual.

- ✓ Judicial Clerkship Handbook, Office of Career Services, University of Michigan, 2007.

  http://www.law.umich.edu/currentstudents/careerservices/Documents/clerk.pdf

  A comprehensive career services guide for students interested in all aspects of clerking, with information about why you should consider it, the variety of clerkships, types of Courts, and a full explanation of the application process and timeline.

- ✓ "Practice in the Federal District Courts from the Clerk's Perspective, the rules being the rules," prepared by Kenneth C. Broodo and Douglas D. Haloftis. 43 *Baylor L.Rev* 333 (1991).

WRITING AND PUBLISHING LAW ARTICLES

- ✓ *Academic Legal Writing: Law Review Articles, Student Notes, Seminar Papers, and Getting on Law Review*, 3d ed. by Eugene Volokh. Foundation Press (2007).

  http://www.law.ucla.edu/volokh/writing/

- ✓ *Choosing a Topic for Your Journal Article: A Guide for University of Minnesota Law Students*, by Suzanne Thorpe. University of Minnesota Law Library Updated August 2007.

  http://www.law.umn.edu/library/pathfinders/choosingatopic.html

- ✓ Dos and Taboos for Making Law Review: A Law Student's Compass, 11 *Crim. Just. J.* 489 (1990) (reprinted in 10 *Legal Reference Services Q.* 149-56 (1990)).

- ✓ How to Write a Law Review Article, by Richard Delgado. 20 *U.S.F. L.Rev.* 445 (1986)

  An often-cited, nuts-and-bolts piece on how to produce legal writings.

- ✓ *Scholarly Writing for Law Students: Seminar Papers, Law Review Notes, and Law Review Competition Papers*, by Elizabeth Fajans and Mary R. Falk. St. Paul, Minn.: West Group, 3rd ed. 2005. For writing law review articles in particular. The advice in this book is helpful for developing a thesis, critiquing authority, and writing with a "voice."

- Stalking the Golden Topic: A Guide to Locating and Selecting Topics for Legal Research Papers, by Heather Meeker. 1996 Utah L. Rev. 917 (1996).

- Writing A Student Article, by Eugene Volokh. 48 *Journal of Legal Education* 247 (1998). (now expanded into an excellent book, *Academic Legal Writing,* cited above)

USEFUL WEB SITES FOR PROSPECTIVE LAW FACULTY

AMERICAN BAR ASSOCIATION
http://www.abanet.org

ASSOCIATION OF AMERICAN LAW SCHOOLS
http://www.aals.org/

BRIAN LEITER'S LAW SCHOOL RANKINGS
http://www.leiterrankings.com/

INSTITUTE FOR HUMANE STUDIES
http://www.TheIHS.org

LAW REVIEW EDITORIAL ADDRESSES OF 101 LAW REVIEWS
Compiled by John Doyle of Washington and Lee Law School.
http://law.wlu.edu/library/mostcited/index.asp

Link to addresses and submissions requirements for each law review. A rank order listing of the 'top' general interest or special interest journals.

THE VOLOKH CONSPIRACY
http://www.volokh.com

COLUMBIA LAW SCHOOL - CAREERS IN LAW TEACHING
http://www.law.columbia.edu/careers/law_teaching

Appendix II:
Success Factors in Legal Academic Careers: Some Survey Data

by David Price, *Institute for Humane Studies*

In March and April of 2007, the Institute for Humane Studies surveyed college and university faculty in five disciplines—economics, history, philosophy, political science, and law—regarding career success factors in their respective fields. We invited 2,648 faculty to take part and obtained 307 completed surveys from tenure-track and tenured faculty.

We received forty-one completed surveys from law faculty—thirty-five tenured faculty and six tenure-track (but not yet tenured) faculty. Although the sample size of law faculty is not large, the results may be of interest to prospective law professors in thinking about career strategy. The results for law were generally consistent with the results from the other disciplines we studied.

We looked at four stages of a typical law professor's career: deciding to become a law professor, obtaining a judicial clerkship, obtaining the first faculty appointment, and obtaining tenure. For each of these stages, we asked respondents to rate a number of factors on a scale of 1 to 5, where 1 means unimportant and 5 means highly important.

Those ratings are shown below. The first number next to each factor is the 1-to-5 rating respondents gave, on average; the second is the margin of error of that average (in more technical terms, the 95% confidence interval). The highest-rated factors are shown in bold face.

I. Deciding to Become a Law Professor

As in other disciplines, law professors reported that the most important influence, on average, on an individual's decision to pursue a career in academia is an interest in ideas—specifically, an interest in academic writing.

"What do you think are the most important influences, pro and con, on an individual's decision to pursue a career as a full-time law school professor?"

Interest in a specific scholarly agenda (3.7 ± 0.3)
Interest in academic writing (4.5 ± 0.2)
Interest in perceived academic lifestyle (3.9 ± 0.3)
Law school loans create pressure to opt for law firm salary (2.7 ± 0.3)
General desire for law firm salary and potential partnership (3.4 ± 0.3)
Willingness to relocate (3.6 ± 0.3)
Lack of interest in traditional legal career (3.8 ± 0.3)

II. OBTAINING A JUDICIAL CLERKSHIP

Law professors (who are often former clerks themselves) perceived that a student's chances of being hired for a clerkship are most strongly affected by the status of the student's law school and by his or her law school grades. A leadership position on a voluntary law journal (that is, a law journal other than the school's main law review) was perceived as having relatively little value in the competition for clerkships.

"What are the most important influences on a law student's or law graduate's ability to obtain an appellate or Supreme Court clerkship?"

High-ranked law school (4.7 ± 0.2)
Law review membership (4.3 ± 0.2)
Law review leadership position (3.7 ± 0.3)
Leadership position on law journal other than main law review (2.7 ± 0.3)
Law school grades (4.8 ± 0.1)
Law school faculty recommendations (4.3 ± 0.2)
Recommendation from "feeder" professor for this judge (4.2 ± 0.3)
Clerked for "feeder" judge on a lower court (4.0 ± 0.3)

III. OBTAINING A FACULTY APPOINTMENT

At law schools, as in other disciplines, a record of publishing journal articles is highly valued in deciding on-campus visits. Also like other departments, law schools place the greatest weight on the quality of the candidate's job talk in deciding whether to extend an offer.

Among the disciplines we examined, law is the *only* one in which a graduate degree in another field appears to be substantially valued in the hiring process. An LL.M. degree reportedly has little value in this regard, though we did not test specialized LL.M. degrees separately from general ones.

"In your field, what are the greatest influences on a candidate's being invited for an on-campus visit for a tenure-track position?"

Performance at AALS conference interview (4.4 ± 0.2)
Expertise in hot/fashionable specialty (3.1 ± 0.3)
Expertise in specialty for which school has curricular need (4.0 ± 0.3)
High-ranked law school (4.2 ± 0.2)
Law review membership (3.6 ± 0.3)
Law review leadership position (3.2 ± 0.4)
Leadership position on law journal other than main law review (2.5 ± 0.3)
Law school grades (4.3 ± 0.3)
Recommendations from former professors (4.1 ± 0.2)
U.S. Supreme Court clerkship (4.2 ± 0.3)
Prestigious federal appeals court clerkship (4.0 ± 0.3)
Other judicial clerkship (2.9 ± 0.3)
DOJ Office of Legal Counsel or Solicitor General's Office (3.2 ± 0.4)
Other federal agency experience (2.4 ± 0.3)
LL.M. degree (1.8 ± 0.3)
Graduate degree in another field (3.7 ± 0.3)
Scholarly publications beyond law review note (4.7 ± 0.2)

"Once invited for an on-campus visit, how do successful candidates (those offered an appointment) tend to distinguish themselves?"

Have stronger resume/pedigree than other candidates interviewed (3.6 ± 0.3)
Project an interest in the school during campus interviews (3.5 ± 0.3)
Project good personality during campus interviews (4.0 ± 0.3)
Show strong substantive knowledge during campus interviews (4.1 ± 0.2)
Show familiarity with interviewers' work during campus interviews (2.6 ± 0.3)
Describe a strong research agenda during campus interviews (4.2 ± 0.2)

Defend controversial positions capably during campus interviews (3.7 ± 0.3)
Deliver quality job talk (4.6 ± 0.2)

IV. OBTAINING TENURE
Scholarly publications in prestigious journals were perceived as by far the most important factor in obtaining tenure at law schools.

"At your institution, what are the most important success factors for a junior faculty member in obtaining tenure?"

Record of publications in prestigious journals (4.6 ± 0.2)
One or more books published with a scholarly press (3.0 ± 0.4)
Student evaluation of teaching quality (3.1 ± 0.3)
Classes are sought-after by students (2.4 ± 0.3)
University service (1.8 ± 0.3)
Filling otherwise-unmet curricular needs (2.3 ± 0.3)
Positive relationships with colleagues (3.6 ± 0.3)
Not having enemies in department (3.2 ± 0.4)
Recommendations from outside professors (3.5 ± 0.3)
Popular/non-scholarly writing (1.6 ± 0.2)

ACKNOWLEDGEMENTS

The Institute for Humane Studies would like to express its appreciation to the faculty who contributed chapters to this guide and to all who were involved in its publication. This edition of *Law School and Beyond* draws substantially from the original edition, which was published in 1999 under the editorship of John Moser.

Eugene Meyer of the Federalist Society provided comments on a draft of the original edition. Mr. Moser also received assistance from then-Dean Mark Grady and professors Frank Buckley and John Hasnas of the George Mason University School of Law, and professor Ward Farnsworth of the Boston University School of Law. The Barre Seid Foundation kindly provided funding for the production of the first edition.

The managing editors of this edition were Christy Rhoton and Tenille Martin. David Price provided editorial guidance. John Schrock, Nigel Ashford, and Jonathan Fortier commented on a draft. Min Shepherd was the copy editor. Eunice Kim designed the book and its cover.

The Institute for Humane Studies

The Institute for Humane Studies was founded in 1961 by Dr. F. A. "Baldy" Harper, a former economics professor at Cornell University. Part of a generation that lived through two devastating world wars and saw the rise of totalitarian dictatorships, Dr. Harper was convinced that greater understanding of human affairs and freedom would foster peace, prosperity, and social harmony.

Dr. Harper founded the Institute for Humane Studies "to further the science of a free society" through research and education. He believed that the principles and practice of a free society require an investigation of all the humane disciplines: history, political science, economics, philosophy, law, literature, art, sociology. So the Institute would be interdisciplinary, would work with scholars and students, and would pursue, through critical inquiry, a better understanding of the free society.

Based for many years in Menlo Park, California, IHS moved in 1985 to northern Virginia to affiliate with George Mason University. With an existing base of market-oriented scholars and centers, GMU provides a setting where the Institute is growing its programs in cooperation with other organizations associated with the university.

Today, with a primary focus on students, the Institute continues the work begun by Dr. Harper. The mission of IHS is to support the achievement of a freer society by discovering and facilitating the development of talented students, scholars, and other intellectuals who share an interest in liberty and who demonstrate the potential to help change the climate of opinion to one more congenial to the principles and practice of freedom.

The Institute offers a variety of programs of education, financial assistance, and career development as well as online intellectual resources. Continuing to uphold the ideals of peace, prosperity, and social harmony, IHS promotes the study and application of liberty across a broad range of disciplines, encouraging open inquiry, rigorous scholarship, and creative problem-solving.